P9-DEM-585

DAVID ELKIND

All
Grown Up
&
No Place
to Go

Teenagers in Crisis

ADDISON-WESLEY PUBLISHING COMPANY

Reading, Massachusetts • *Menlo Park, California*
London • *Amsterdam* • *Don Mills, Ontario* • *Sydney*

Permission has been granted to use the following material:

Selections from *Then Again, Maybe I Won't* by Judy Blume, reprinted by permission of Dell Publishing Co. (New York, 1971).

"Cecilia Rosas," by A. Muro, from *The New Mexico Quarterly* (Winter 1964–1965).

Library of Congress Cataloging in Publication Data

Elkind, David, 1931–
  All grown up and no place to go.

  Bibliography: p.
  Includes index.
  1. Youth—United States. 2. Adolescent psychology—
United States. 3. Stress (Psychology) I. Title.
HQ796.E535 1984   305.2'35   84-6388
ISBN 0-201-11378-3
ISBN 0-201-11379-1 (pbk.)

Cover design and photograph by Marshall Henrichs
Set in 11-point Palatino by Techna Type, Inc., York, PA

ABCDEFGHIJ-DO-8987654
First printing, April 1984

Contents

*T*o my beloved wife, Nina,
whose strength during the dark times,
patience during the trying times, and
wisdom, loyalty, and love at all times
are woven into every sentence

Acknowledgments

A book is always written alone, in the privacy of one's work room. But the writer also carries in his or her head all of the many collaborators who contributed facts, thoughts, ideas, challenges, support, and criticism. The writing time is like the slender part of the hourglass, where all the collected thoughts have to go through one narrow channel, a single mind, before they return to the larger population from which they came. It is not possible to thank all my collaborators by name. First and foremost are the teenagers I have known and worked with over these many years. Then there are the parents, sometimes busting their buttons, sometimes angry, and sometimes just outright scared. And there are the many teachers and administrators who have taught me so much about young people's lives in their homes away from home—the schools. And finally I have to acknowledge the health professionals, nurses, social workers, physicians, psychologists, and psychiatrists who give so much of themselves to the children and youth they serve. To all of you, my thanks and appreciation.

I also want to thank my former departmental assistant, Louise Clancy, for typing an early draft of the book and Dorothy O'Toole, who typed later versions. Susan Oleksiw and Kendra Crossen provided valuable editorial help on the manuscript. And I want to thank my three adolescent sons, Paul, Robert, and Rick, for teaching me how easy it is to give advice and how hard it is to follow it. And I owe much to my two stepsons, Carl and Walter, for being such ardent and loyal supporters. Last but not least I want to thank the editors at Addison-Wesley: Doe Coover, who worked with me on the first draft, and Anne Eldridge, who took over from there and saw the book through its final stages. Both were unfailing in their support and encouragement.

David Elkind
South Yarmouth, Massachusetts
March 1, 1984

Preface

Over the past twenty-five years I have worked with young people in many different settings. I have worked with teenage patients at psychiatric hospitals and with delinquent teenagers who were being brought to court. I have also seen teenagers who came with their families to child guidance clinics or to my private practice. And, with colleagues, I have conducted research with students who were attending junior and senior high school. That research often involved interviewing large numbers of young people. I have reported my observations and concerns about teenagers in articles, book chapters, and books for professionals and for parents. I know, and care, about young people.

Over the past two years, however, I have had a very different kind of interaction with teenagers, with their parents and teachers, and with professionals in many different fields who provide for their health needs. With the publication of an earlier book, *The Hurried Child*, I had many requests to speak from all parts of the United States and Canada. I have now traveled to every state in the Union and to all the Canadian provinces. Everywhere I go, I make it my practice not only to speak but also to listen.

What I have heard, and what I am hearing, was the impetus for writing this book. Not only are children still being hurried, but the phenomenon is becoming more common and accepted.

Mothers-to-be are deluged with literature assuring them that if they use the right materials they will be able to raise their babies' I.Q. and have them reading, swimming, and doing gymnastics before they are three months old. There is, of course, no evidence to support the value of such early pushing. There is, however, considerable evidence that children are showing more and more serious stress symptoms than ever before.

Even more discouraging has been the realization that many of these hurried children are now teenagers. Now, more than a decade after the hurrying began, we are getting a truer measure of the cost of acceleration as we look at the threefold increase in stress symptoms among young people. What I have seen and heard is frightening enough. Many parents and many schools and much of the media have been hurrying children to grow up fast, but they have also been abandoning teenagers. There is simply no protected place for teenagers in today's hurried and hurrying society.

The result is a staggering number of teenagers who have not had the adult guidance, direction, and support they need to make a healthy transition to adulthood. We always lost a certain number of teenagers in the past, for all kinds of reasons. But we are losing too many teenagers today. We are producing too many young people who may never be productive and responsible citizens, much less lead happy and rewarding lives. When 50 percent of our youth are at one or another time abusing alcohol or drugs, then something is seriously wrong with our society.

That is why I wrote this book. The one encouraging experience I had, wherever I traveled, was meeting many parents, teachers, and health professionals who are deeply committed to young people and who really care. But they need help and support to continue and to resist the social pressure to foist a premature adulthood on teenagers. This book is written for them—and for all the teenagers whom I have known and worked with over the past quarter of a century.

Part I

Needed:
A Time to Grow

Chapter 1

Teenagers in Crisis

*T*here is no place for teenagers in American society today—
not in our homes, not in our schools, and not in society
at large. This was not always the case: barely a decade ago,
teenagers had a clearly defined position in the social structure.
They were the "next generation," the "future leaders" of America. Their intellectual, social, and moral development was considered important, and therefore it was protected and nurtured.
The teenager's occasional foibles and excesses were excused as
an expression of youthful spirit, a necessary Mardi Gras before
assuming adult responsibility and decorum. Teenagers thus
received the time needed to adapt to the remarkable transformations their bodies, minds, and emotions were undergoing.
Society recognized that the transition from childhood to adulthood was difficult and that young people needed time, support,
and guidance in this endeavor.

In today's rapidly changing society, teenagers have lost
their once privileged position. Instead, they have had a premature adulthood thrust upon them. Teenagers now are expected to confront life and its challenges with the maturity once
expected only of the middle-aged, without any time for preparation. Many adults are too busy retooling and retraining their
own job skills to devote any time to preparing the next generation of workers. And some parents are so involved in reor-
dering their own lives, managing a career, marriage, parenting,

and leisure, that they have no time to give their teenagers; other parents simply cannot train a teenager for an adulthood they themselves have yet to attain fully. The media and merchandisers, too, no longer abide by the unwritten rule that teenagers are a privileged group who require special protection and nurturing. They now see teenagers as fair game for all the arts of persuasion and sexual innuendo once directed only to adult audiences and consumers. High schools, which were once the setting for a unique teenage culture and language, have become miniatures of the adult community. Theft, violence, sex, and substance abuse are now as common in the high schools as they are on the streets.

It is true, of course, that many parents and other adults are still committed to giving teenagers the time, protection, and guidance they require to traverse this difficult period. But these well-meaning adults meet almost insurmountable barriers in today's society, and many feel powerless to provide the kind of guidance they believe teenagers need. For example, a mother of a teenager asked me recently what to do with her fourteen-year-old son who was staying up late to watch X-rated movies on cable television. I suggested that if she did not want him to see the movies, she should not permit him to do so and should give him her reasons for the prohibition. Her next question surprised me. She asked me what she should do if he watches them after she goes to bed. It was clear that the mother felt helpless to monitor her son's TV watching. For this youth, as for many others, premature adulthood is gained by default.

In today's society we seem unable to accept the fact of adolescence, that there are young people in transition from childhood to adulthood who need adult guidance and direction. Rather, we assume the teenager is a kind of adult. Whether we confer premature adulthood upon teenagers because we are too caught up in our own lives to give them the time and attention they require or because we feel helpless to provide them with the safe world they need, the end result is the same: teenagers have no place in this society. They are not adults capable of carrying the adult responsibilities we confer upon them. And they are not children whose subservience to adults can be taken for granted. We expect them to be grown up in all those domains where we cannot or do not want to maintain control. But in other domains, such as attending school, we expect our teenagers to behave like obedient children.

Perhaps the best word to describe the predicament of today's teenagers is "unplaced." Teenagers are not displaced in the sense of having been put in a position they did not choose to be in (a state sometimes called anomie). Nor are they misplaced in the sense of having been put in the wrong place (a state sometimes called alienation). Rather, they are unplaced in the sense that there is no place for a young person who needs a measured and controlled introduction to adulthood. In a rapidly changing society, when adults are struggling to adapt to a new social order, few adults are genuinely committed to helping teenagers attain a healthy adulthood. Young people are thus denied the special recognition and protection that society previously accorded their age group. The special stage belonging to teenagers has been excised from the life cycle, and teenagers have been given a pro forma adulthood, an adulthood with all of the responsibilities but few of the prerogatives. Young people today are quite literally all grown up with no place to go.

The imposition of premature adulthood upon today's teenagers affects them in two different but closely related ways. First, because teenagers need a protected period of time within which to construct a personal identity, the absence of that period impairs the formation of that all-important self-definition. Having a personal identity amounts to having an abiding sense of self that brings together, and gives meaning to, the teenager's past while at the same time giving him or her guidance and direction for the future. A secure sense of self, of personal identity, allows the young person to deal with both inner and outer demands with consistency and efficiency. This sense of self is thus one of the teenager's most important defenses against stress. By impairing his or her ability to construct a secure personal identity, today's society leaves the teenager more vulnerable and less competent to meet the challenges that are inevitable in life.

5

The second effect of premature adulthood is inordinate stress: teenagers today are subject to more stress than were teenagers in previous generations. This stress is of three types. First, teenagers are confronted with many more freedoms today than were available to past generations. Second, they are experiencing losses, to their basic sense of security and expectations for the future, that earlier generations did not encounter. And third, they must cope with the frustration of trying to prepare for their life's work in school settings that hinder rather than facilitate this goal. Any one of these new stresses would put a heavy burden on a young person; taken together, they make a formidable demand on the teenager's ability to adapt to new demands and new situations.

Contemporary American society has thus struck teenagers a double blow. It has rendered them more vulnerable to stress while at the same time exposing them to new and more powerful stresses than were ever faced by previous generations of adolescents. It is not surprising, then, to find that the number of stress-related problems among teenagers has more than trebled in the last decade and a half. Before we examine in more detail the predicament of today's teenagers, we need to look at some of the frightening statistics in order to understand both the seriousness and the magnitude of the problem.

A Generation under Stress

Substance abuse is now the leading cause of death among teenagers and accounts for more than ten thousand deaths each year. Although the use of drugs has leveled off after a threefold rise in the last decade and a half, alcohol use is becoming more widespread and is appearing among younger age groups. According to a recent survey of junior high school students, 65 percent of the thirteen-year-olds had used alcohol at least once that year, some 35 percent used it once a month, and 20 percent used it once a week. Thirty-five percent of the thirteen-year-olds queried said that it was fun and all right to get drunk. The

National Institute on Alcohol Abuse and Alcoholism reports, conservatively, that 1.3 million teenagers between the ages of twelve and seventeen have serious drinking problems. According to a 1981 report from the Department of Health, Education and Welfare, more than three million youths nationwide have experienced problems at home, in school, or on the highways as a result of drinking.[1] In my own travels throughout this country I have found that it is commonplace for beer to be available at parties for twelve- and thirteen-year-olds. It is often provided by parents, who, relieved that the youngsters are not into drugs, appear to consider alcohol benign by comparison.

Sexual activity, at least among teenage girls, has more than tripled over the last two decades. In contrast to the 1960s, when only about 10 percent of teenage girls were sexually active, more than 50 percent are sexually active today. By the age of nineteen at least 70 percent of young women have had at least one sexual experience. Among young women who are sexually active, four out of ten will become pregnant before they leave their teens. Currently about 1.3 million teenagers become pregnant each year, and more than a third of them are choosing to have and to keep their babies.[2] Although young women may be able to conceive an infant, the pelvic girdle does not attain its full size until the age of seventeen or eighteen. This puts the young teenage mother and her infant at physical risk. The data also indicate that the infants of teenage mothers are more at risk for child abuse and for emotional problems than are the children of more mature mothers.

Suicide rates for teenagers have climbed at a fearful pace. Five thousand teenagers commit suicide each year, and for each of these suicides fifty to one hundred youngsters make an unsuccessful attempt.[3] Sex differences in mode of suicide are changing. Girls, who in the past resorted to pills and slashing their wrists, are now using the more violent means often employed by boys, namely, hanging and shooting. In addition, many "accidental" teenage deaths are regarded by experts as being, in part at least, suicidal.

Crime rates have increased dramatically among juveniles.

For many children, crime is a regular part of their lives, in both the home and the school.

> Every month, secondary schools experience 2.4 million thefts, almost 300,000 assaults and over 100,000 robberies. Criminal behavior starts early, usually in school, and peaks quickly. More 17 to 20 year old males are arrested for virtually every class of crime (including homicide) than males in any other age group. But the record of children under 10 (55,000 arrests in 1980) is itself sobering and it gets seven times worse by age 14.[4]

To these alarming statistics we must add that over one million children run away from home each year, and an indeterminate number of these are forced into prostitution or pornography, or both.[5]

These statistics define the gravity of the problems resulting from teenage stress. Now we need to examine some of the social changes that have taken place in this country and how they have led us to deny, ignore, or abdicate our responsibilities toward youth.

Social Change and Teenage Identity

It is generally agreed today, following the original work of the psychoanalyst Erik Erikson, that the primary task of the teenage years is to construct a sense of personal identity.[6] In Erikson's view, the teenager's task is to bring together all of the various and sometimes conflicting facets of self into a working whole that at once provides continuity with the past and focus and direction for the future. This sense of personal identity includes various roles (son or daughter, student, athlete, musician, artist, and so on), various traits and abilities (quiet, outgoing, timid, generous, high-strung), as well as the teenager's personal tableau of likes and dislikes, political and social attitudes, religious orientation, and much more.

It is clear from this description that the task of forming an identity is a difficult and complex one. It is not undertaken until the teen years in part because the young person has not accumulated all the necessary ingredients until this time, and in part because prior to adolescence young people lack the mental abilities required for the task. The late Jean Piaget demonstrated that it is not until the teen years that young people are capable of constructing theories.[7] And it is not unreasonable to characterize identity as a theory of oneself. Forming an identity, like building a theory, is a creative endeavor that takes much time and concentrated effort. That is why Erikson has suggested that teenagers either make or find a "moratorium," a period of time for themselves during which they can engage in the task of identity formation.

In the past, a clearly demarcated period of development, called adolescence, gave young people the needed respite before assuming adult responsibility and decision making. But this period is no longer available. The current generation of young people is being denied the time needed to put together a workable theory of self. The issue, it should be said, is not one of leisure or free time. Many teenagers today have that. Rather, what is lacking is *pressure-free* time, time that is free of the burdens designated properly for adults. Even at their leisure teenagers carry with them the adult expectation that they will behave as if they were already fully grown and mature. It is because young people today carry with them, and are often preoccupied by, adult issues that they do not have the time to deal with properly teenage concerns, namely, the construction of a personal definition of self.

It is not only time that is missing. Teenagers also need a clearly defined value system against which to test other values and discover their own. But when the important adults in their lives don't know what their own values are and are not sure what is right and what is wrong, what is good and what is bad, the teenagers' task is even more difficult and more time-consuming. The process of constructing an identity is adversely affected because neither the proper time nor the proper ingredients are available. Let us consider how the very process of identity formation is affected by the teenager's being "un-placed" in the society.

Social Change and Parenting

In the last thirty years our society has undergone more change, at a faster rate, than during any other period. We are now moving rapidly from an industrial to a postindustrial or information society:

> Twenty-five years ago, the nation's work force was about equally divided between white-collar and blue-collar jobs, between goods and service industries. There are now more people employed full time in our colleges and universities than are employed in agriculture. In 1981, white-collar jobs outnumbered blue-collar jobs by three to two. And the number of people employed by U.S. Steel is smaller than the number of employees at McDonald's.[8]

The nature of the work force has changed as well. Over half of the 25 million women with children in the United States are working outside the home, compared with 20 percent in 1950.

Although the changes relating to work are significant, even greater changes have come about in our values and social philosophy. Daniel Yankelovich has likened this shift to the major changes in the earth's crust as a result of shifts of the tectonic plates deep in the earth's interior. Yankelovich argues that we are rapidly moving away from the "social role" orientation that once dominated American society.[9] He describes the old "social role" (give-and-take) philosophy this way:

> I give hard work, loyalty and steadfastness, I swallow my frustrations and suppress my impulse to do what I would enjoy, and do what is expected of me instead. I do not put myself first; I put the needs of others ahead of my own. I give a lot, but what I get in return is worth it. I receive an ever growing standard of living, and a family life with a devoted spouse and decent kids. Our children will take care of

us in our old age if we really need it, which thank goodness we will not. I have a nice home, a good job, the respect of my friends and neighbors, a sense of accomplishment at having made something of my life. Last but not least, as an American I am proud to be a citizen of the finest country in the world.[10]

That is the philosophy most of today's parents grew up with, and it is the one most adults today recognize as familiar and generally their own. But over the last twenty years a new philosophy has emerged to vie with the older social role orientation. This new philosophy has been variously called the "culture of narcissism" or the "me generation" or more kindly by Yankelovich as a "search for self-fulfillment." According to numerous surveys by Yankelovich and others, this new philosophy now fully pervades our society:

By the late seventies . . . seven out of ten Americans (72 percent) [were] spending a great deal of time thinking about themselves and their inner lives, this in a nation once notorious for its impatience with inwardness. The rage for self-fulfillment . . . has now spread to virtually the entire U.S. population.[11]

The changes we are undergoing today in American society have been described in somewhat different terms by John Naisbitt in his book *Megatrends*.[12] He argues that the "basic building block of the society is shifting from the family to the individual" and that we are changing from a "fixed option" to a "multiple option" society. Choices in the basic areas of family and work have exploded into a multitude of highly individual arrangements and life-styles. And the basic idea of a multiple option society has spilled over into other important areas of our lives: religion, the arts, music, food, entertainment, and, finally, the extent to which cultural, ethnic, and racial diversity are now celebrated in the United States. Both Yankelovich and Naisbitt suggest that there are many pluses and minuses to the new self-fulfillment philosophy, just as there were for the social role orientation. Moreover, it may be, as Naisbitt suggests, that an individual-oriented social philosophy is better suited than a role-oriented social philosophy to the requirements of an information society.

However that may be, the important point here is not that one philosophy is good and the other is bad, but rather that we as adults and parents are caught in the crossfire of these two social philosophies. Sexual values are a case in point. As parents and adults, we have the values we learned as children; as members of a modern society, we recognize that values have changed and a new set of values is followed. The conflict arises when we as adults must confront the new values rather than merely tolerate them. Recently a father admitted to me that his daughter is living with a man. The father grew up when I did, and at that time a young woman who lived with a man would most probably be disowned by her family. But such behavior is the norm today, and though the father may feel deeply that what his daughter is doing is wrong, the contemporary value system supports it. After all, isn't everyone else doing it? This father must now cope with two conflicting value systems—his own and his daughter's.

Parents who, like this father, would like to protect and shield their offspring feel overwhelmed by the pressure to accept the new social code. If they openly challenge the new values, they are sure to be labeled, and dismissed, as old-fashioned and stuffy. Ellen Goodman put the dilemma of the committed parent in a time of changing values this way:

> I belong to a whole generation of people who grew up under traditional rules about sex. We heard all about the rights and wrongs, shoulds and shouldn'ts, do's and don'ts. As adults we have lived through a time when all these rules were questioned, when people were set "free" to discover their own sexuality and their own definition of morality. Whether we observed this change from the outside or were part of it, we were nevertheless affected by it. Now, with all of our ambivalence and confusion, we are the new generation of parents raising the next generation of adults. Our agenda is a com-

plicated one, because we do not want to be the new guardians of sexual repression. Nor are we willing to define sexual freedom as the children's right to do it. We are equally uncomfortable with notions that sex is evil and sex is groovy.[13]

In times of rapid social change, even committed parents are confused about what limits to set and what values to advocate and to enforce. For us adults this is a time to give serious thought to our values and principles, just as it is a time to struggle for greater tolerance. Ironically, our responses may only make matters worse for teenagers. Caught between two value systems, parents become ambivalent, and teenagers perceive their ambivalence as license. Failing to act, we force our teenagers to do so, before they are ready. Because we are reluctant to take a firm stand, we deny teenagers the benefit of our parental concern and we impel them into premature adulthood. We say, honestly, "I don't know," but teenagers hear, "They don't care."

Parents who are themselves awash in the tide of social change and are looking for self-fulfillment may have a different reaction to the teenager. A parent going through a "midlife" crisis may be too self-absorbed with his or her own voyage of personal discovery to appreciate fully and support the needs of a teenage son or daughter. Similarly, parents who are undergoing a divorce (as more than one million couples a year do) may be too caught up in the turbulence of their own lives to be of much help to a teenager with his or her own kind of life change. Other parents, who may be learning new job skills such as those involved in using computers, may look upon teenagers as having the advantage. Such parents may feel that the teenager has more knowledge and technological sophistication than they have and therefore that teenagers have it made. It may be hard for these parents to see the teenager's need for a special time and for support and guidance.

Still other parents and adults find the pace of social change too much to take and are overwhelmed by it. While their mates may have found the new social philosophy liberating and challenging, they find it frightening and isolating. If divorce comes,

13

they feel adrift and alone, lost in a world they did not bargain for and do not want to participate in. It is a great temptation for these parents to reverse roles and look to their teenagers for support and guidance. Here again, the impact of social change is to deny the teenager the time and freedom to be a teenager in order to prepare for adulthood; the teenager is rushed from childhood to adulthood in order to meet the needs of a troubled parent.

Rapid social change, particularly from one social philosophy to another, inevitably affects parental attitudes toward teenagers. Although different parents are affected in different ways, the end result is always the same. For one reason or another, in one way or another, teenagers are denied the protection, guidance, and instruction they desperately need in order to mature. As we shall see in later chapters, it is not only parents but society as a whole that is unplacing teenagers. Perhaps this is why Hermann Hesse in *Steppenwolf* described the plight of youth caught between social philosophies in this way:

> Every age, every culture, every custom and tradition has its own character, its own weaknesses and its own strength, its beauties and ugliness; accepts certain sufferings as matters of course, puts up patiently with certain evils. Human life is reduced to real suffering, to real hell only when two ages, two cultures and religions overlap. . . . Now there are times when a whole generation is caught in this way between two ages, two modes of life with the consequence that it loses all power to understand itself, and has no standard, no security, no simple acquiescence.[14]

If we put Hesse's last sentence in contemporary terms, we would say that youths caught between two cultures have a weak sense of identity (no standard, no security) and self-definition and are thus more vulnerable to stress. Clearly our situation today is not unique; there have been comparable periods in history. But that does not make our present situation any more tolerable. Today's teenager must struggle to achieve a sense of self, a sense of personal identity, if she or he is going to go on to build a full life as a mature and complete adult. But by bestowing a premature mantle of adulthood upon teenagers, we as parents and adults impair the formation of their sense of identity and render them more vulnerable to stress. We thus endanger their future and society's as well.

Two Ways of Growing

When we talk about a "mature" person, we are talking in part about the healthy sense of identity and of self developed during the teen years. This sense of personal identity is constructed by one of two methods, either by differentiation (the process of discriminating or separating out) and higher-order integration (or simply integration) or by substitution. The kind of parenting a teenager receives and the social climate in which he or she grows up are critical in determining which of these two paths of development a young person will follow, and what sort of self-definition he or she will attain.

Growth by *integration* is conflictual, time-consuming, and laborious. A child who is acquiring the concept of squareness, for example, must encounter a variety of different shapes before he or she can separate squareness from roundness or pointedness. In addition, the child must see many different square things such as boxes, dice, sugar cubes, and alphabet blocks before he or she can arrive at a higher-order notion of squareness that will allow him or her to differentiate a square from all other shapes and to integrate all square things, regardless of size, color, or any other features, into the same concept.

The principles of differentiation and integration operate in the social realm as well. To acquire a consistent sense of self, we must encounter a great number of different experiences within which we can discover how our feelings, thoughts, and beliefs are different from those of other people. At the same time, we also need to learn how much we are like other people.

We need to discover that other people don't like insults any more than we do and that other people appreciate compliments just as we do. As a result of this slow process of differentiating ourselves from others, in terms of how we are alike and yet different from them, we gradually arrive at a stable and unique perception of our self.

Once growth by integration has occurred, it is difficult if not impossible to break down. After a child has acquired the concept of squareness, for example, he or she will not lose it; the concept becomes a permanent part of the self and a consistent way of seeing reality. The same is true in the social realm. People who have a strong sense of self do not lose it even under the most trying circumstances. Survivors of concentration camps and of brainwashing had such strong concepts of self that even extreme stress, exposure, starvation, torture, did not break them.

Mental structures achieved by differentiation and integration also conserve energy and reduce stress. Once we know what a square is we can identify it immediately; we don't have to go through a laborious process of differentiation and integration in order to recognize it again. In the same way, once we have an integrated sense of self, we know what to do in different situations. A well-defined sense of self and identity provides us with effective strategies for managing psychological stress—the major stress in our society. Later, in Chapter 8, we will look at three basic stress situations and how a healthy sense of self and identity enables us to cope with them effectively and with a minimum expenditure of energy.

The second way in which growth occurs is by *substitution*. Consider the transition we have all made from making a phone call by turning a wheel several times to getting the same number by pushing buttons. Learning to dial a number by turning a wheel is not a preparation for getting that number by pushing buttons. Both actions have the same result, but the first skill is neither required to learn the second nor incorporated within it. Both exist independently and side by side. Either skill can be drawn upon if needed. This type of learning is clearly of value, particularly in a society with a rapidly changing technology. In adapting to new technology, it is an advantage to be able to replace old habits quickly with new ones.

The same principles, again, can be followed in social growth. Indeed, substitution is the kind of growth suggested by the well-known adage "When in Rome do as the Romans do." In some social situations, particularly those in which we don't know the rules, it is generally considered wise to adapt and to follow the example of others who are familiar with the situation. But such learning is not adaptive when it comes to constructing a sense of personal identity. A sense of self constructed by the simple addition of feelings, thoughts, and beliefs copied from others amounts to a *patchwork* self. A person who has constructed a self in this way is not in touch with the deeper core of his or her being. Young people who have a self constructed by substitution are easily swayed and influenced by others because they do not have a clear definition of their own self. In addition, they are more vulnerable to stress than teenagers with an integrated sense of self because each new situation is a new challenge. Teenagers with a patchwork self have not developed an inner core of consistency and stability that allows them to deal with new situations in terms of past experiences.

These two different kinds of growth account for the two quite different types of teenagers we see. Teenagers who have acquired an integrated sense of identity are able to postpone immediate gratification in order to attain long-range goals. They are future-oriented and inner-directed. In contrast, teenagers who have grown by substitution and have only a patchwork self are less able to postpone immediate gratification. They are present-oriented and other-directed, easily influenced by others. By encouraging teenagers to choose growth by substitution and the development of a patchwork self, contemporary society has rendered teenagers more vulnerable to stress and denied them the full development of their personality and character.

The foregoing is the basic argument of this book: there is no place for teenagers in today's society; consequently teenagers are made more vulnerable to stress at the very time when they are being exposed to more powerful stress than ever before. Before elaborating this theme, we need to look at how teenagers have been treated in the past in order to clarify how we are treating them today.

Teenagers Today and Yesterday

The conception of youth as an important and well-marked stage of development dates from antiquity. This idea, however, has had a cyclical history. It seems to have been recognized and emphasized, and then lost and forgotten, only to be rediscovered at a later time. Ancient Greece was one point in history where adolescence was clearly marked. Aristotle, for example, described young people in remarkably familiar terms: "Young men have strong passions and tend to gratify them indiscriminately. Of the bodily desires, it is the sexual to which they are most disposed to give way, and in regard to sexual desire they exercise no self-restraint."

During the Dark Ages the conception of stages of development and of adolescence as a unique stage was lost and a theological theory of human nature was advanced. This theory was that of the homunculus, a "little man" already fully formed in the male sperm. It was believed that when this homunculus was implanted in the woman, the homunculus merely grew in size until the full-term fetal size was attained at the end of nine months. From the standpoint of the homunculus theory, the difference between children and adults was a simple matter of quantity: the adult was larger than the infant and more experienced, but in every other way they were roughly equal.

The homunculus theory was soon challenged by the scientific thinkers of the Renaissance. Once scientific observation came to be a criterion of truth, it was noted that children have both qualitative and quantitative characteristics of their own and are not miniature adults. During this period the stage of adolescence was rediscovered, if not widely accepted and appreciated. During the succeeding period, the age of "Enlightenment," there was a growing appreciation of the stage of youth as a period of *Sturm und Drang*, of "Storm and Stress."

Among the most renowned of the Enlightenment writers was Jean Jacques Rousseau, whose classic *Emile* was the beginning of modern child psychology and progressive education.[15] Rousseau, like Aristotle, believed that development occurred in a sequence of stages. Rousseau's third stage, ages thirteen to fifteen, was concerned with the development of reason and self-consciousness. His notion that youths were inherently decent and were corrupted by an immoral adult society was the opposite of the prevailing religious view that they were, by nature, imbued with original sin and that it was the task of the church and of God-fearing adults to save them. A century later, Charles Darwin added a new dimension to this controversy when he introduced his theory of evolution. By placing humans on the evolutionary ladder with animals, this theory removed humans from their special religious category. Darwin's work thus gave a new scientific legitimacy to the conception of adolescence as a stage, more than two millennia after the idea was articulated by Aristotle.

Darwin's work was the foundation upon which the social sciences were built. As long as human beings were considered outside nature, as part of a religious category, they could not be studied by scientific means any more than religious dogma could be tested empirically. But once humans were regarded as part of nature, their behavior, both individually and collectively, was open to study. Social science, psychology, sociology, and anthropology flourished in the remaining decades of the nineteenth century after Darwin's work was first published. The study of children and adolescents was part of this explosion of new knowledge, which has continued to this day.

Adolescence in America

Belief in the significance of adolescence as a distinct stage in the life cycle emerged in this country when we moved from an agricultural to an industrial economy. On the farm, parents saw children as smaller and weaker adults who could help with the difficult labor of the farm. This notion of children as small adults persisted into the beginning of the industrial revolution when children were used as cheap labor in the factories. But as industrialization and mechanization progressed, children and adolescents were no longer needed in the job market. Parents, who were factory laborers now, began to see children as in need of education and technical training to prepare them for a factory economy. The response of adults to children during the industrial revolution is perhaps the most obvious example of how the economy shapes parental attitudes toward children and youth.

The fact that children were no longer needed in the labor force, along with a more humanistic attitude toward them (reflecting the new view that such handicaps as retardation and mental illness had natural rather than divine causes), led to a series of new child labor laws. By 1914 almost every state in the nation had laws prohibiting the employment of youth below a certain age, usually fourteen. The removal of teenagers from the main labor force was a clear sign of their special estate. As Edgar Friedenberg wrote:

> Adolescence is conceived as a distinct stage of life in those societies so complicated and differentiated that each individual's social role and function takes years to define and to learn. When years of special preparation for adult life are required, these years become a distinguishable period with its own customs, rules and relationships.[16]

The special place of teenagers in society was also recognized by those concerned with education. To function in an industrial society, young people had to know how to read and write and had to have basic information and skills in science and mechanics. In addition, they had to be conditioned to the rhythms of factory work, which is different from farm work. Farm work follows the rhythms of the calendar, the changing seasons. Factory work follows the rhythms of the clock and, with the miracle of artificial lighting, allows work to continue at any time of the day or night. Schools in their schedules—in the taking of the roll, in the sounding of bells to signal entrance time and dismissal, and in the short lunch hour—patterned themselves after factories and in this way prepared young people for the rhythms of factory work. Being a "student" or a "pupil" marked young people as being in a special apprenticeship position in society.

As the years passed and the stage of adolescence became more fully accepted and better understood, more legislation concerning juveniles gradually emerged, this time concerned with drinking (and later driving), voting, and legal responsibilities of all sorts.

The social rediscovery of adolescence in the United States was thus both a reaction to economic needs and a reflection of parental attitudes engendered by the new knowledge about adolescence provided by social science. The result of the rediscovery was the recognition that in a highly industrialized society, young people needed a period between childhood and adulthood, a period before the final assumption of adult responsibilities and decision making. Parents, teachers, the media, the church, the government, and industry all agreed and supported this need of youth and defined the life of the adolescent accordingly.

The recent denial of adolescence as a special stage of life is therefore a denial of more than a century of growth in our understanding of youth. It is, quite literally, a return to the concept of the homunculus theory held during the Dark Ages. We hurry young people as children and then unplace them as teenagers. We cannot, dare not, persist on this dangerous course of denying young people the time, the support, and the guidance they need to arrive at an integrated definition of self. Teenagers are the next generation and the future leaders of this country. Their need is real and pressing. We harm them and endanger the future of our society if we leave them, as our legacy, a patchwork sense of personal identity.

Chapter 2

Thinking in a New Key

Adjusting to new ways of thinking is one of the most difficult tasks confronting teenagers. This is not an obvious fact. Indeed, we adults tend to assume that adjusting to physical changes is what gives teenagers the most trouble, especially since those changes are so noticeable as boys and girls grow rapidly taller, change quickly in body configuration, and show dramatic changes in facial structure (the nose growing before the chin, for example). Accordingly, when young people show irritability, sullenness, and other signs of stress, it is understandable that we attribute such reactions to the trauma of rapid physical growth.

Yet even more dramatic than the physical changes are the mental changes, which often appear first. In adolescence, one develops the ability to think on a higher level, to think in a new way. The new thinking abilities are like a Copernican revolution in the way young people see themselves, others, and the world in general. And these new thinking abilities strongly color how young people adjust to the changes in their bodily configuration and appearance. For example, the self-consciousness so common in the early teen years is a result of a change in thinking and not just a product of the physical changes (or lack of them) themselves. In a letter asking for help, a boy named George reflects his new awareness of the need for peer-group approval, not just his concern about physical immaturity:

> Help, I don't have any pubic hair that shows. The boys call me "Baldy" and the girls want to know why, and it's so embarrassing. I'm fourteen. Shouldn't I have it by now?[1]

It is George's new mental powers that bring about the change in the way he reacts to the physical transformations of puberty. George has conceived a standard of physical development and is disturbed that he does not seem to measure up. He is very concerned about what his peers think about him. Both concerns derive from his thinking in a new key.

It is important to remember that young people are as unfamiliar with their new thinking abilities as they are with their newly reconfigured bodies. Moreover, thinking on a higher level takes time to get used to. Teenagers need to become accustomed to thinking in a new key, just as they need to become accustomed to living in a new body. And just as they are often awkward in the use of their transformed bodies, they are sometimes equally awkward in the use of their new thinking powers. As adults we have to be careful not to mistake their awkwardness in thinking, which may sometimes manifest in the form of insensitive remarks, for anything more sinister than inexperience.

Formal Operational Thinking

Since ancient times, the age of six or seven has been known as the age of reason, for it was the age at which children began to use logic in their thinking. It was Jean Piaget, however, who pointed out that a second age of reason appears in adolescence.[2] This new mode of reasoning brings with it a higher mode of logic. In contrast to the syllogistic reasoning of the school-age child, the young adolescent can employ the logic of propositions and truth tables. This new level of reasoning enables teenagers to deal with possibilities, with what might be rather than with what is. If, for example, you say to a child, "Let us

24

suppose that coal is white," the child will object, "But it is black." The teenager, in contrast, can accept the contrary-to-fact condition as a purely logical proposition that can be reasoned about regardless of its factual truth.

Piaget gave the name "formal operations" to the ability to engage in propositional thinking. These operations enable young people to go beyond the here and now, to grasp historical time and celestial space, to comprehend abstract subjects like philosophy, algebra, and calculus, and to appreciate simile, metaphor, and parody. In many different respects, therefore, these operations enable teenagers to think on a more abstract level.

A personal anecdote may help to illustrate this mode of thinking. Some years ago, when my sons were younger, we were sitting at the dinner table and my oldest son, Paul, who was thirteen at the time, was talking about a book he was reading, Tolkien's *The Hobbit*. His brother, Rick, who was then eight, misheard Paul and asked, "What is a Hobble?" In a rare moment of comic inspiration I made what I thought was a hilarious joke. I said, "Rick, a Hobble is a Hobbit with a sore foot." Paul laughed, not hilariously, but Rick did not get the joke. I had, of course, made a pun, a play on words, which Rick did not yet understand because he had not yet attained formal operations. The understanding of puns, like the understanding of metaphor and simile, irony and sarcasm, all rest upon the attainment of propositional logic. This logic enables young people to recognize that words can have both literal and suggestive meanings.

Mad magazine, beloved at first by older teenagers, has now been adopted by young teenagers, who appreciate its satire. Children younger than eleven or twelve cannot really enjoy some of the *Mad* humor exemplified in the modified commercials that are one of *Mad*'s specialties:

> Star Wars Mouthwash—Destroys Bad Breath
> I'd give up an Empire for it

> After chomping down that big meal . . .
> Pac Man Antacid Tablets for gas

25

Miss Piggy Kosher Franks
Très Kosher—Take it from me[3]

To understand the double meanings of these parodies, the reader must be capable of the propositional logic made possible by formal operations. A pun may be the lowest form of wit, but enjoying it requires the highest level of intelligence, which emerges in adolescence.

One reason young people enjoy word play so much is that it allows them to practice their new mental abilities at the same time that it enables them to express their antipathies for certain aspects of the adult world. In word play they are learning to define their own tastes, values, and preferences in a constructive way. With their new intellectual abilities, adolescents can use humor to explore and define aspects of themselves that may be too delicate or inchoate to be examined in the light of cool logic.

In their humor, as in many other features of their thinking, boys and girls begin to show differences that were latent during childhood. We really don't know to what extent these differences are culturally conditioned and to what extent they represent more basic sex differences. They do exist. Consider the kind of humor in this passage from *Matthew Looney and the Space Pirates*, a book read primarily by boys:

> "Don't say I didn't warn you," Matt signaled the two Royal Moonties. They moved over and grabbed Herton's arms.
> "Just a moonit," he said, trying to shake loose. "If I don't go then you don't go neither."[4]

Even in early adolescence, boys' humor tends to be more direct and obvious than the humor enjoyed by girls. Compare the foregoing passage with the one below from a book read primarily, if not exclusively, by girls. This is how Margaret in Judy Blume's book *Are You There God? It's Me, Margaret* responds to a new male teacher's questionnaire used to find out more about his students.

26

My name is: Margaret Ann Simon
Please call me: Margaret
I like: Long hair, tuna fish, the smell of rain and things that are pink.
I hate: Pimples, baked potatoes, when my mother's mad, religious holidays.
This year in school: I want to have fun.
I think male teachers are: The opposite of female teachers.[5]

Teenagers can use puns, metaphors, sarcasm, and satire without fully realizing they are using an allegorical mode of speech. The colorfulness of teenage language comes from this spontaneous and creative use of metaphor, simile, and parody. Consider the following statements, which were made as natural, satirical expressions of two teenagers' self-evaluations:

Why can't I look as chic as Alice? I look like the Salvation Army dresses me.[6]

I'm too tall, and I'm still growing. I'm only twelve and I'm the tallest person in the whole seventh grade. I look tall and feel tall too. Is there anything I can do to stop growing? —Giraffe.[7]

Boys often use their new-found powers of inventing similes and metaphors to devise terms that will embarrass well-endowed girls, who may be called Stack House or B.B. (Big Boobs). Less well-endowed girls are not neglected; they may be called Boards or N.B. (No Boobs).

As these examples make clear, teenagers' new mental abilities transform and color the way they deal with their changing bodies and their social relationships. In the following pages we will look at other ways in which young people's new intellectual abilities affect the way they think about themselves and others and the way in which they relate to adults and to peers. All of these new interactions require time to work out and to get used to, for everyone involved.

Idealism and Criticalness

Formal operations enable young people to go beyond the real to the possible, and this opens up the world of the ideal and of perfection. For the first time teenagers can imagine a world of peace and harmony, a perfect church and a perfect family. The criticalness of parents that emerges in early adolescence derives, in part, from the teenager's ability to imagine ideal parents against whom his or her real parents suffer by comparison. Some teenagers even engage in what has been called a foundling fantasy. The fantasy is that they were adopted and that their real parents are nobility, extremely wealthy, or very famous.

The new criticalness of parents often happens rather abruptly. The pleasant and obedient ten-year-old, a pleasure to parents and teachers alike, does not prepare the unsuspecting adults for what is to come. As young people move into formal operations, their once respectful, obedient approach to parents may be transformed into something quite different. As one mother wrote in a letter to the *Boston Globe*:

> Buba is now the ripe age of 11. Yesterday my husband and I received a note from her (a common form of communication around here when one is particularly upset) that was so mature and such a plea for understanding that we both wept at the passing of our little girl.
>
> In it she thanked us for all of the wonderful things we have done for her (good opening, lull parents into feeling good) and then hit us right between the eyes, the old one-two about never listening and never understanding and blaming her for everything and yelling too much and feeling left out of the family and not being sure if we loved her too much (if at all), take a breath for effect, what are we going to do about it?[8]

Buba's new-found intellectual capacity was clearly a challenge to her parents. She now looked at them with a critical or discerning eye and pointed out their blemishes to them. Boys, whose physical development is a little later than girls', may

28

develop a little more slowly intellectually as well. But when the new mental abilities appear, the criticism is sure to follow. Sometimes, of course, the criticism is implied. Here is how one young man in Jeanne Betancourt's book *Am I Normal?* saw his father's reactions to questions about sex:

Here goes. I sit on the edge of the chair opposite him, "Dad?"

He looks up real nice and says, "Yes son?" like I'm about to ask him if he wants another dish of ice cream. I look at the floor. "Dad, can you tell me about, uh, sex?"

He zaps off the TV and swivels his rocker toward me all concerned. "What's the matter, John? Are you in trouble or something?"

"Trouble? No, Dad. I'm not in any trouble." I look up at him. "I'm in confusion. Nobody at school seems to know what's going on and a lot of crazy stories are going around. I thought you could . . ."

"Oh . . . I see. You want to know about . . . sex?"

I nod.

"That's terrific, son. Just between you and me, right? Man to man, father to son. You know my father never talked to me about . . . that kind of stuff. Okay, let's see now . . ."

Finally some answers. I told you he wouldn't laugh.

Dad leans forward and so do I. We're eye to eye, man to man.

"Son, it's like this," says Dad, shifting in his seat. "Men have, uh, their own baseball bats."

He frowns for a second and tries again. "No, no, that's not it." He continues, "Um, girls have catcher's mitts and boys have a, well, no . . ."

Poor Dad is wiggling like crazy in his easy chair. He keeps glancing back at the blank TV screen. We are no longer eye to eye.

"Am I helping you son?"

"Not really. It's just that,"

He interrupts. "Okay, let's do this, John. There's first base, second base and,"

"No, Dad. I mean, what about all those changes that are going on in my body and everything?"

"Changes?" That word makes him more uncomfortable than sex did.

He picks up the remote control. "Son, men just know these things. That's all, they just know. It'll come to you. You'll see. Don't worry about anything. Now I'm gonna watch my game."[9]

Sometimes, of course, the criticism is much less subtle and indirect. The respectful, loving eleven-year-old becomes the disrespectful, critical twelve-year-old. Suddenly, a boy who never washed, changed his shirt, or used a fork without a battle becomes a connoisseur of manners, dress, and behavior. Out of the blue, as it were, parents are told that they do not know how to walk, how to talk, how to dress, how to eat. My own parents were Russian immigrants. But this never bothered me until I became a teenager and discovered, as if I had never heard them speak before, that they had accents. They also did not dress like my friends' American-born parents. (My mother's hair came to the floor and she wore it in two long braids wound together to make a bun at the back of her head.) I remember now, not without some shame and regret, how critical I was of them at the time and how embarrassed I was to introduce them to my friends.

There is another aspect to this criticalness that comes from a different, more primitive kind of thinking. When teenagers start having crushes on young people of the opposite sex, this causes problems in their relationship with their parents. Many teenagers believe that love comes in a fixed amount and that each person has only so much to give. If you have only a pound of love, and half of it belongs to your mother and half to your father, where is the love you feel for this "awesome" boy or girl going to come from? Clearly it has to be taken from the portions allotted to the parents. When teenagers have a crush, they experience it as taking something away from what they owe or should be giving to their parents.

Not surprisingly, when this happens, the young person feels guilty. After all, the parents have taken care of the teenager all of these years and are entitled to their half-pound of love apiece. Or are they? One way to resolve the issue without feeling guilty, helped by the ability to imagine ideal parents, is to find fault with the parents. If they are unloving, insensitive, demanding, and so on, they are not nice, not deserving of their half-pound of love apiece. By measuring parents against an ideal, the teenager can see that parents are less than perfect, and therefore the teenager is justified in withdrawing some love from the parents and giving it instead to a friend of the opposite sex.

The value and importance of this process of measuring parents and others against abstract standards usually appear much later. Teenagers who have learned to see people they love as both lovable and flawed have a much greater capacity for positive and rewarding relationships as adults. During the adolescent years, the teenager's critical remarks about his or her parents provide an opportunity for positive growth by letting the teenager see himself or herself in contrast with other personalities. Although parents should not take these criticisms too seriously, they should also not go unanswered. Various responses are suitable: "I am very happy with the way I am, so I guess you will have to accept it; that's what growing up is all about." Or "Okay, I am willing to listen to your complaints if you will give me equal time to voice my complaints about you." Such remarks can help young people differentiate their point of view from that of their parents. It can help them to recognize that their parents can be as unhappy with them as they are with their parents.

Argumentativeness

As teenagers acquire formal operations they are motivated to use and practice them. This is true for children at all levels of development. Recall the four-year-old who is learning to count. This child will ask repeatedly, "Do you want to hear me count to a thousand?'' And he or she will do so at the slightest invitation. Children spontaneously practice their emerging mental abilities. But teenagers now have the ability, thanks to formal operations, to marshal facts and ideas and to make a case. Unlike children, who tend to see things as black or white, good or bad, right or wrong, adolescents begin to see shades of gray, degrees of goodness and badness, and gradations of rightness and wrongness. As a result, teenagers will no longer settle for the parental dictate, ''Do it because I tell you to,'' which might suffice for a child. Rather, they want to know the reasons they should or should not do something. And then, when they are given an explanation such as, ''You can't go out because it is a school night and you have homework to do and you need to get up early,'' they may argue back, ''But I have done most of my homework and I can do the rest in study hall and I can't fall asleep early anyway.'' Such arguments, while painful for parents, have to be seen for what they are—namely, an effort by the young person, in part at least, to use and exercise his or her new powers of argument.

Indeed, parents of teenagers often tell me, ''But he [or she] argues for the sake of arguing.'' I tell them that they are absolutely correct. It is not just the issue—staying out late, for instance—that prompts the teenager to argue, but the need to argue for the sake of arguing. Once we recognize that fact we can handle the matter in a way that will promote constructive growth. We can help adolescents to distinguish between argument as an exercise in logic and argument as an attempt at persuasion. Young people need to argue, but we can argue with them about principles, not about emotional positions. Homework should be done because it is part of going to school and the obligations and responsibilities to which a student commits himself or herself. Teenagers may want to argue these principles, and that is fine. What you want to do is leave motivation and personality out of the discussion. By eliminating emotionally charged subjects from the areas available for argument, we give teenagers the practice they need without upsetting ourselves and teach them to differentiate the process of argument from the uses to which it can be put.

32

Self-Consciousness

Another characteristic of the young teenager that results directly from thinking in a new key is self-consciousness. Formal operations make it possible for young people to think about thinking. Children think, but they don't think about thinking. For example, in a study I conducted on children's conception of their religious denomination, I asked, "Can a dog or a cat be Protestant (or Catholic or Jew, depending upon the denomination of the child)?"[10] Regardless of religious denomination, children said that a dog or a cat could not be a Protestant, Catholic, or Jew because the minister, priest, or rabbi would not allow the animal in the church or the synagogue. "They would make noise and run around!" one child explained.

Teenagers, on the other hand, uniformly offered a different answer: "They are not intelligent; they would not understand religion." Others said, "They don't believe in God." Concepts like "intelligence" or "understanding" or "belief" are ideas about thinking that children rarely use but teenagers use with increasing frequency. Teenagers can think about thinking, about what goes on in their heads and what goes on in the heads of others.

Because teenagers are caught up with the transformations they are undergoing—in their bodies, in their facial structure, in their feelings and emotions, and in their thinking powers—they become self-centered. They assume that everyone around them is concerned about the same thing they are concerned with, namely, themselves. I call this assumption the *imaginary audience*. It is the imaginary audience that accounts for the teenager's extreme self-consciousness. Teenagers feel that they are always on stage and that everyone around them is as aware of and as concerned about their appearance and behavior as they themselves are.

All of us retain some imaginary audience fantasies even when we are fully grown. I recall eating alone in a large restaurant in a strange city. I accidentally dropped my knife, which hit the marble floor with what sounded like, to me at any rate, an ear-rending clang. For a moment I was sure that everyone

33

was looking at me and thinking, "What a klutz!" Some adults even become dependent upon the imaginary audience. The fading motion picture star may become depressed because he or she is sure the audience will see every new wrinkle, gray hair, and blue vein. Other men and women, puffed up with their success, are sure that everyone is watching them at a restaurant, where they loudly call the headwaiter by his first name, make a show of being put at the best table, and so on. More generally, the contemporary concern with designer labels is clearly a concern with impressing an audience that, in honesty we have to admit, is largely imaginary.

In fact, if the truth were told, we as actors are in the audience's consciousness for only a brief moment, if at all. Most people spend almost all of their time thinking about their own lives, their own problems, their own hopes and frustrations. Of course, people admire a strong performance or someone who is successful in his or her field, but these ideas occupy an infinitesimal part of most people's waking thoughts. That insight, however, usually comes later in life, if at all, and young teenagers stubbornly believe that they are the focus of everyone's abiding attention and concern. Hence they are very self-conscious and often go to extreme lengths to avoid what they are convinced will be mortifying experiences. In the following fictional passage from Paula Danziger's, *The Cat Ate My Gymsuit,* a sensitive overweight girl handles the problem of avoiding gym in a manner that speaks poignantly of the teenager's sometimes overwhelming new self-consciousness.

> I just sat there. Trying to change into a gymsuit while hiding my mini bra and fat body would have been a gymnastic feat in itself.
>
> Once the class started, I walked up to the gym teacher, Schmidt.
>
> "All right, Lewis, what is it this time?"
>
> "The cat ate my gymsuit."
>
> She shook her head, frowned and wrote another zero in her marking book.
>
> I sat down to watch my eighty millionth volleyball game.[11]

For this teenage girl, as for many others, the imaginary audience looms so large that she has to get off the stage.

The imaginary audience helps us to understand several otherwise puzzling changes in teenagers' behavior. For example, how are we to explain the boy for whom every request to take a bath or to put on fresh clothing once provoked a battle and who then, overnight it seems, begins spending hours in the bathroom, bathing and combing his hair? When they stand in front of a mirror, teenagers imagine the audience's reaction to their appearance. They are also much more sensitive about public exposure. That is why it is so important for adults who deal with young teenagers to avoid public criticism and ridicule. If we have to correct a teenager about something, it is imperative that we wait until we can speak to him or her alone.

As teenagers grow older, their concern with the imaginary audience tends to diminish; through broader experiences and expanded social relationships they come to focus less on themselves. This change has been demonstrated in several studies using an Imaginary Audience Scale.[12] The scale consists of items such as, "You have been looking foward to going to a party for over a month. Once you arrive, after an hour-long drive, you discover a grease spot on your slacks or skirt. Do you stay or return home?" The results from the several studies tend to be fairly consistent. Most preteens seemed unconcerned and said that they would go to the party anyway. Similarly, older teenagers (sixteen to seventeen years) generally answered, "They are my friends, no one would care." But many young teenagers (thirteen to fourteen years) said they would go home or stand in a dark corner or pour something on themselves to explain the spot.

Clearly the imaginary audience reflects the teenager's inability to differentiate between his or her own preoccupations and those of others. We can best help teenagers make these differentiations if we take a middle ground between accepting the teenager's view of the world and completely rejecting it. If a teenage girl says that she has a blemish on her cheek, she is ugly, and the whole world knows she is ugly, we won't get far if we try to reassure her that she is pretty. Nor will she appreciate it if we agree with her assessment that she is ugly. If we take a middle position, we might say, "Well, you certainly don't look ugly to me, but that is my opinion. What do other people do? Do they say things to you, make faces, what?" In this way we encourage the teenager to test the audience fantasy against reality. This testing of the fantasy against the reality helps the teenager to differentiate between the way he or she might like the world to be and the way it really is. The teenager learns judgment and objectivity while being free of the tyranny of the imaginary audience.

Self-Centeredness

Perhaps because teenagers are so convinced that people are observing and thinking about them, they get an inflated opinion of their own importance. They begin to feel that they are special and unique. The teenage boy who is sure that the pretty girl at the party is looking at him in a special way reflects this kind of thinking. Another teenager may believe that her admired teacher really likes her better than the other students in the class but just doesn't show it. I have called this assumption of specialness the *personal fable*. It is a story that we tell ourselves but that isn't true. We tell ourselves, "Other people will grow old and die, but I won't" or "Other people won't realize their life ambitions, but I will realize mine."

Like the imaginary audience, the personal fable, in a simplified form, stays with us for the rest of our lives. It is our legacy from adolescent thought. Given all the dangers of contemporary life, we would hardly venture outside our homes if we did not clothe ourselves in a personal fable, a shield of invulnerability. It is the fable that convinces the soldier going into battle that the other men will be killed or wounded; he will survive. Quite simply, the fable gives us hope.

The fable is much more prominent in adolescence than at any other stage in life. For example, a teenager may keep a diary with the expectation that it will one day be published as the great American novel that everyone has been waiting for. Or a girl may tell her mother, "Mom, you don't know how it feels to be in love." In both cases the young person gives the impression that his or her experience is unique and special. Revising the fable in a realistic way is a part of maturing, of slowly developing a distinct sense of self, and continues throughout our lives. When I was a youth, my mother suffered a heart attack, and I had to come to grips with my own fable. Serious illness happened to other people's parents, to other families, not to mine. It wasn't right somehow; I was supposed to be protected. Only when I confronted my assumption of invulnerability was I able to master my anxiety and help my mother cope with her illness. Thank God, she recovered.

Sometimes the fantasy of the imaginary audience and the fable work together, as when young people believe they are special in an undesirable way and everybody knows about it.

> Cheryl Ladd, for example, thought she was too busty as a teenager and she even held her schoolbooks in front of her to conceal what she believed was her problem. Or, when fourteen-year-old Valerie Bertinelli first appeared as Barbara Cooper on "One Day at a Time" she felt insecure about her body and was critical of her looks. "I felt fat and ugly," she recalled.[13]

Young teenagers tend to believe that they are the only ones who are concerned about their bodies and that other adolescents, even if they have more serious problems, are better able to cope than they are. The fable contributes not only to our feeling that our problems are unique but also to the conviction that our experiences are unique as well:

> In the deep facet way in which feeling becomes stronger than thought, I had always felt that Devon School came into existence the day that I entered it, was vibrantly real while I was a student there and then blinked out like a candle on the day I left.[14]

In short, the fable can suggest to us that we are special in both a positive and a negative way. Our problems are special; no one else has it so bad. But our joys are special too; no one else has it so good.

The personal fable stays with us, being modified now and again according to new experiences but always present in our lives as part of our definition of ourselves. The process by which the fable changes through the years is the same one used to develop the sense of personal identity: differentiation and higher-order integration. Not surprisingly, teenagers consider the fable to be similar to an unalterable truth, and we should not challenge the fable head on. Such an approach will only entrench teenagers in their position. Arguing with someone else's reality simply does not work.

Rather than argue with young people about how much they are like other people (a denial of their fable), we as adults can point out that other people are special, too. A parent can say, "Your father is a very special person; he works very hard to give us the life we have and never, ever complains." Or "Your mother is a very special person; she manages a career, looks after us, and still has time for friends and recreation." We do not have to deny the teenager his or her uniqueness in order to assert our own. By emphasizing the uniqueness of all people, we can help teenagers distinguish between the ways in which they are alike and the ways in which they are different from other people.

Decision Making

Teenagers, particularly young teenagers, have trouble making decisions. It is agony to decide what to wear, what to eat, sometimes even what to say. This indecision is again the result of the teenager's ability to think in a new key. Teenagers who can think in propositions can keep so many ideas in mind simultaneously that they have trouble choosing among them. In this respect, a teenager is a little like the child at the candy store who can see so many different kinds of candy that it is impossible to make a choice. The teenager, in effect, carries the candy store around in his or her head, making the problem much more persistent. He or she is repeatedly faced with the questions of how and what to choose.

When teenagers are forced to make decisions, they often come up with choices that may seem bizarre. Clothing is the most obvious example in the eyes of most adults. A girl who doesn't know what to wear to school will ask her mother for advice and then choose the opposite of her mother's suggestions. A boy will insist on wearing a jacket when it is hot and on taking it off when it is cold because he is "boiling." Food provides another example. Many young people become addicted to fast-food places because they require very few decisions. Once a teenager decides on a preferred menu—hamburger, large Coke, small fries, cherry pie—the problem of choice is solved for now and eternity. A restaurant menu, in comparison, provides so many choices that the teenager will usually revert to his or her preferred menu and order something as close to the fast-food meal as possible.

The difference between the teenager and the adult in this area is the amount of experience in making decisions; as a result of this experience the adult has acquired some rules and strategies for making decisions. In regard to clothing, for example, some people dress according to their mood, some use a rotation method (a different color combination each day), and some dress according to the calendar—Brown Monday, Blue Tuesday, and so on. When adults have little experience, however, they may behave like teenagers. Detroit may have lost much of its business to foreign automakers in part because it gave the new car buyer too many choices. Foreign automakers, in contrast, provided cars that were "fully equipped," with limited options. They thus eliminated the need for complex decisions on the part of the buyer. It is true, of course, that people buy foreign cars for other reasons, but the absence of difficult decision making in purchasing a foreign car does add to its attractiveness.

It is not just experience, strategies, and rules that help us to make decisions; we also use emotional cues. In choosing what to wear, what to eat, where to go for entertainment, we listen to our feelings. If we are feeling depressed, we may want to wear something with a bit of dash to counteract the mood. If we feel like celebrating, we may choose to go to a really nice restaurant. If we are feeling lonely, we may want to see a romantic comedy to revive our spirits. Teenagers, however, are not in close touch with their feelings in the sense of being able to distinguish and label them. Moreover, their moods change with such rapidity that choices made on the basis of the feeling of one moment may not be suited to the emotions of the next moment. As a result, there is often a lack of fit between the teenager's decisions and feelings that can be disconcerting to adults. For example, the teenager who is feeling depressed may go to see a sad movie.

With experience teenagers become better able to recognize their different moods and feelings. With time and increasing maturity, the rapid emotional swings will subside. We can help teenagers discriminate between some of their feelings by suggesting to them how they might be feeling. A concerned parent might say, "You are looking a little down. Would you like to go shopping with me or join us for a movie?" Helping young people to recognize and understand their feelings is every bit as important as helping them do the same with their thoughts.

Apparent Hypocrisy

Young people become very idealistic once they have attained the level of formal operational thought. Although they are usually vocal in expressing their ideals, they often fail to carry out the actions that would seem to follow logically from their professed ideals. To use an expression from my own youth, they don't put their money where their mouth is. Unfortunately, this often means that young people seem like hypocrites to adults, who can see considerable discrepancy between the ideals teenagers espouse and the efforts they are willing to expend to realize those ideals.

There is, however, only an apparent hypocrisy. Again let me use a personal example to illustrate both the appearance of hypocrisy and the developmental truth that underlies it. When I was living in Rochester, New York, there was a program called Walk for Water. It encouraged junior and senior high school students to find adults who would pledge a certain amount of money (usually a quarter per mile) for every mile the teenager chose to walk. The money earned in this way was used to support various local environmental causes. I had made a pledge and was driving along the route of the march on a Sunday morning on my way to the airport. All along the road there were thousands of young people walking in an orderly manner, singing in unison. My impression was, "What a great bunch of kids!" At that moment I had a renewed faith in the youth of the country and in our hopes for a better future. Unfortunately for my new-found optimism, I returned along the same route the next day. Now there were crews cleaning up the debris of Coke cans and bottles, McDonald's hamburger wrappers and boxes, napkins, straws, and so on. It probably cost the city more, I thought, to clean up the mess than the kids raised by their march.

It would be easy, but incorrect, to call these teenagers hypocritical. Rather, they simply did not recognize the difference between expressing an ideal and working toward it. Young people believe that by expressing a value they are working toward its realization. To the younger teenager, expressing an ideal, by marching or another means, is all that one really has to do. The expression is enough. If they express an ideal by verbalizing it or by marching and parading banners, that should suffice for its realization. If it is not realized once it expressed, then it must be someone else's fault. And that someone else usually happens to be the corrupt adults over thirty. It is only when young people engage in meaningful work that they begin to differentiate between the expression of an ideal and the hard work necessary to bring it to fruition. Encouraging teenagers to get jobs, even paying them to do chores we might pay someone else to do around the house, is one way that we as parents

and concerned adults can help teenagers grow in their understanding of the relationship between imagining a goal and
working to make it a reality.

Personal Religion

Parents are not the only ones who suffer by comparison with
the ideal; religions also suffer. The child who went to church
or synagogue without question now understands that religion
is more than an activity and that it involves belief. Teenagers
begin to distinguish between institutional religion, which is
social, and personal religion, which is private. Children, for
example, don't distinguish clearly between the prayers they
may say at church and those they may say at home. In both
situations they are essentially asking for something. But teenagers suddenly become aware of institutional religion with its
priesthood, vows, doctrines, practices, and taboos, and the
personal God who is in effect nondenominational and available
to them at all times. It is the God we all refer to at times of
crisis; it is the same for the soldier in the foxhole, the frightened
parent in the hospital, the patient facing terminal illness. But
teenagers, who value their privacy—now that they have discovered that they can live in secret in their heads—and who
are afraid that their secrets might be found out, discover that
a personal God is a most trustworthy confidant. He won't squeal.

The teenage distinction between institutional and personal
religion is nicely illustrated in Judy Blume's *Are You There God?
It's Me, Margaret*. Margaret comes from a mixed marriage and
is trying to decide which religion to adopt as her own:

> Are you there God? It's me, Margaret. I just came home
> from Church. I loved the choir, the songs were so beautiful.
> Still I don't feel you, God. I'm more confused than ever. I'm
> trying hard to understand but I wish you would help me a
> little. If only you could give me a hint, God. Which religion
> should I be? Sometimes I wish that I had been born one way
> or the other.[15]

For Margaret, there is no difficulty in admitting confusion or uncertainty to God. Some young people may reject institutional religion entirely when they become teenagers. In a way they are saying, "I'm too old. I don't believe in that stuff anymore." It is also a way of rebelling against (or differentiating themselves from) parents and religious authority. But teenagers very much need a religious element in their identity. Having a religious faith, of whatever denomination, even if the teenager does not practice it, gives him or her a known quantity, a fixed ingredient, to integrate into his or her developing definition of self.

In general, most young people return to the faith of their parents once they become young adults and particularly when they become parents. But others, given the stresses encountered in today's society, may join cults that offer a quick and easy solution to life's problems. As parents and caring adults, we can help young people most by encouraging a religious orientation when they are children and acknowledging their need for a period of time free of institutional religion when they are teenagers. At this time, both the religious institution and parents should move away from religious instruction and provide opportunities for the social interaction and discussion of values, beliefs, and actions that young people need to discover who and what they really are. Such a sabbatical from institutional religion prepares the way for a later integration of personal and formal religious beliefs and values.

Chapter 3

Perils of Puberty

C hildren fret, teenagers worry. Children fret about what they can and cannot have, where they can and cannot go. Teenagers worry about themselves, about what they will look like once they pass through puberty, about the future. Worry is a new emotion made possible by their new ability to think in a new key. Young people begin to worry when they become capable of anticipating the future (a product of formal operational thinking), and puberty provides not one but rather a whole series of matters to worry about. As soon as one issue is resolved, another takes its place. If teenagers are not worried about height, they are worried about weight; if not menstruation, then breast size; and so on. Puberty presents teenagers with a series of unknown changes, and each one constitutes a peril of puberty.

Worrying about the perils of puberty is a symptom of the stress connected with defining a personal identity. When a girl worries about whether she will ever get her period, she is concerned about being different from her friends who have already "got it." Similarly, a boy who worries about being short is worrying about being different from the norm of attractiveness, strength, and masculinity. He worries about not being included in sports, about being treated as younger than his peers, and about being called names such as "Shorty." The changes associated with puberty are overwhelmingly stressful because they confront the teenager with so many questions difficult to answer. The teenager wonders, "How am I different? How am I the same?" This is only to say that healthy growth, growth by differentiation and hierarchical integration, is stressful in itself and is far from being an easy and simple transition to adulthood. But the short-term stress has a long-term gain: the stress helps young people develop a strong definition of self that is an abiding defense against all forms of stress encountered later in life.

Perils for Girls

For girls, the perils of puberty include the unknowns about the future of their bodies—height, weight, menstruation, breast development, hair growth, body shape and configuration, facial features, skin conditions, and much more. Each aspect is a cause of considerable worry and concern. Some girls handle these concerns by focusing entirely on one aspect. A girl picks breast configuration, for instance, concentrates all of her anxieties and fears on this one feature. She then laments, "If only my breasts were smaller [or larger or firmer], all of my problems would be solved and I would be happy for ever and ever." I call this strategy finding an emotional *lightning rod*. When a girl takes this approach, the feature in question becomes super-charged, capturing the emotions that might be spread over several physical features. If she has focused on breast size, any remark remotely associated with breasts may send her into unspeakable ecstasy or sink her into the dungeons of depression. Breast size becomes a symbol of all the perils (stresses) of puberty; and the teenager's reactions to allusions to breasts becomes, in Freudian terms, *overdetermined*, because her responses erupt from a concentration of intense emotions.

Height and Weight

The perils of puberty begin for girls around the age of nine or ten, when physical growth begins to accelerate. Until this

46

age, there is little difference between boys and girls in height, weight, or strength; both boys and girls have reached about four-fifths of their adult height and somewhat more than half of their adult weight.[1] But as young people move into puberty, the relative uniformity of growth in childhood explodes into a fireworks of different growth rates. Some kids shoot straight up, some have delayed fuses, and some hardly get off the ground at all. Although 95 percent of all girls show at least one sign of puberty between the ages of nine and thirteen and a half, it is still normal for some girls to face their first peril after age thirteen.

On the average, the adolescent growth in height begins for girls at age ten and one-half and ends at age fourteen. By age fourteen most girls have attained their adult height. Some girls, of course, continue to grow beyond that age but seldom beyond age fifteen. Self-consciousness about height may be one of the first teenage concerns if the girl feels she is above or below average. A recent survey of teenagers suggests that 56 percent are not satisfied with their bodies and that one major concern is being "too short."[2]

Changes in the amount and distribution of body fat also occur at puberty. Soon after birth babies begin to accumulate fat just beneath the skin, which gives them their plump appearance. By one year of age most girls have more baby fat than boys. From then until about age seven, both boys and girls begin to lose fat so that by the age of seven many children may look thin and scrawny. Then matters change once more, and most girls and many boys begin accumulating fat again; this can lead to prepubescent chubbiness and the beginning of self-consciousness.

As girls begin their growth spurt, they begin to lose fat again, particularly from their thighs and legs. Even so, girls lose less fat than boys during this time and thus leave the teen years with more fat beneath the skin than boys. It is for this reason that girls have a more rounded shape than boys, who have more muscle and less fat than girls. Boys also appear more muscular because there is less fat to conceal bones and muscle.

Although there is some evidence that a tendency to be

overweight can be inherited and that early overfeeding can contribute to this tendency, most heavy teenagers are over-weight because they eat too much. Unfortunately, for many teenagers, overeating becomes part of a vicious cycle. They are unhappy because they are overweight and eat to feel better, but this only adds to the overweight condition, unhappiness, and the desire to eat to compensate. Some young women do grow out of it, but the waiting is painful:

> My name is Marcy Lewis. I'm thirteen years old and in the ninth grade at Dwight D. Eisenhower Junior High School.
> All my life I've thought I looked like a baby blimp with wire frame glasses and mousy brown hair. Everyone said that I'd grow out of it but I was convinced that I'd become an adolescent blimp with wire frame glasses, mousy brown hair, and acne.[3]

For an adolescent girl newly aware of her body and its now embarrassing imperfections, facing the teen years with a weight problem can seem an interminable misery.

Breast Development

The first visible sign of approaching puberty is the growth of breasts. This may begin between the ages of eight and thir-teen and is usually completed between the ages of thirteen and eighteen, the average being about age fifteen.[4] Breast devel-opment occurs in stages, beginning with the elevation of the nipple and surrounding area (breast bud stage). Next the breast as a whole enlarges and the areola (colored area around the nipple) widens and deepens in color; then the areola develops and forms a secondary contour. Finally, the areola becomes part of one common breast contour. Perhaps because of the breast fetish of American culture, aided by the *Playboy* center-fold, teenage girls are extraordinarily sensitive about their breast development. It is one of the most worrisome perils of puberty for girls. The question of what to do about "unsatisfactory" breasts occurs regularly among teenagers. The following question is typical:

> I'm fourteen years old and I'm flat. I have less on my top than any other girl in my whole class. I was wondering, is there any exercise I can do, or stuff I can send for to make me bigger? —Flat as a Board.[5]

In addition to worries about breast size, girls also worry about their two breasts being of equal size. It is quite normal for one breast to be larger than the other initially, and in almost all cases the other breast catches up and the vast majority of girls end up with a "matched pair." Dr. Maryanne Collins, pediatrician and specialist in adolescent medicine, has pointed this out: "When a young girl starts to develop breasts, one side always enlarges first. Invariably mothers and daughters get concerned because they do not realize that this is normal."[6]

For some girls the perils of puberty are of a different order. A girl whose breasts develop early is subject to the comments and stares of older boys and men as well as to teasing and harassment from other girls. Following from Judy Blume's book, *Are You There God? It's Me, Margaret,* is an interchange between two classmates, Laura and Margaret. Laura matured early. The peril of standing out physically is clearly as dangerous as being a "board."

> "I heard all about you and Moose Freed," I whispered.
> Laura put down her pencil and looked at me. "You heard what about me and Moose Freed?"
> "Oh, about how you and Evan and Moose go behind the A&P," I said.
> "What would I do that for?" Laura asked.
> She was really thick. "I don't know what you do it for. But I know why they do it . . . they do it so they can feel you or something and you let them."
> She shut the encyclopedia hard and stood up. Her face was burning red and I saw a blue vein stick out in her neck. "You filthy liar! You little pig." Nobody ever called me such names in my life.

Margaret pursues Laura and tries to make amends.

> "I didn't mean to insult you," I said. "You are the one who started it."
>
> "Me, that's a good one! You think it's such a great game to make fun of me, don't you?"
>
> "No," I said.
>
> "Don't you think I know about you and your friends? Do you think it is fun to be the biggest kid in the class?"
>
> "I don't know," I said. "I never thought about it."
>
> "Well, try thinking about it. Think about how you would feel if you had to wear a bra in fourth grade and how everybody laughed and how you always had to cross your arms in front of you. And about how the boys called you dirty names just because of how you looked."[7]

Body Hair

Soon after the first signs of breast development occur, another peril emerges: body hair. Like breast development, the appearance of body hair can have positive and negative effects on how young women think about themselves. The first appearance of pubic hair may be taken as a sign of long-awaited maturity and looked upon as one less cause of worry. On the other hand, if body hair growth is extensive, on the arms, legs, and upper lip as well as in the pubic area and beneath the arms, girls can become alarmed at this "unattractive" feature. This attitude is clearly a reflection of our cultural values. Certain physical qualities are considered attractive and others are not. The concern with body hair, for example, is not prevalent in many European countries, where women do not shave their underarms or legs. The use of deodorants to counteract body odor (associated with the growth of hair and the activity of oil-producing glands) is also not common in European countries. Nonetheless, in our society, excess body hair is looked upon as unattractive, and girls who develop this trait often worry about it.

Menarche

Perhaps the most noted or notorious peril of puberty is menarche, the onset of menstruation. In some societies this is made a public event, but in our society it is a private family affair. It is often a later event, usually occurring about two years after breast development and after the peak period of the growth in height. At this time in the United States, the average age of menarche is 12.8 years, but the range is from 9 to 18 years.[8]

Attitudes toward menarche are tied to social values and taboos, which vary over time. In an earlier era in our history menarche was described as "the curse" and was portrayed to young girls as a malady that had to be endured. This attitude often led to some embarrassing moments for young girls:

> What an adventure going out to Illinois at the age of thirteen. . . . But I felt awfully upset, which I supposed was just my excitement at going away. Then of course, it proved to be the curse, for the first time. I thought I was dying of tuberculosis, which in a vague way I knew caused hemorrhages. It must be a serious case because the hemorrhage had gone the wrong way. I wondered if they would find me dead in the car in the morning. I guess they must have told the porter to take special care of me because I'd rather die than call for help. Presently he asked me through the curtain if I was all right. I said, "I guess I'm sick." "What seems to be the trouble, lady?" To that I made no answer at all. I couldn't. With the intuition of a great gentleman, he must have guessed for soon after, a large black hand came through the curtain and handed me a package.[9]

At that time in history (the turn of the century), menarche was very much a private matter, but behind the silence was a tacit understanding of the needs of the adolescent that could make the experience less difficult. The society that protected the teenager from premature adulthood also guided and paced her steps toward maturity. In America today there is no place for a gradual progress toward womanhood, and girls seem to be in open competition to get "it" as soon as or before their friends. For young girls today, menarche is a sign of belonging rather than of growth. Listen to Margaret in Judy Blume's, *Are You There God? It's Me, Margaret,* describe her feelings when her friends have started to menstruate and she is still waiting:

> Are you there God? It's me, Margaret. Gretchen my friend got her period. I'm so jealous, God. I hate myself for being so jealous, but I am. I wish you'd help just a little. Nancy's sure she's going to get it soon, too. And if I'm last I don't know what I'll do. Oh please, God, I just want to be normal.[10]

Once a teenager starts to menstruate, she may still be irregular until the processes of ovulation are well established. Because of this, girls are relatively infertile for a few years after menarche, but this does not amount to contraceptive security. Once the process of ovulation has begun, pregnancy is always a possibility.

Once girls have begun to menstruate and breast development is noticeable, their attention turns to other matters of appearance that are coming to the fore, such as body shape, facial features, and acne. Each new change is agonized over and worried about. And once the pubertal changes are over and girls move into the middle and later teen years, they begin to worry about personality traits such as shyness. In the middle and late teens, the perils of puberty are more psychological than physical. We will examine some of these psychological issues in the next chapter.

Perils for Boys

Puberty presents as many perils for boys as it does for girls. Boys worry about how tall they will become, about when they will have to shave, about the size of their penis, about spontaneous erections, about wet dreams, and about acne. Boys, like girls, sometimes focus all of their worries on one particular physical feature, such as height or large feet (referred to in one family as the British Fleet). They become supersensitive about this particular issue because it represents all the other changes they are anticipating, changes they have no control over and are terribly anxious about. When parents or younger siblings touch on this concern, an explosion of feeling is likely to occur. Everyone is astounded because the response seems so out of proportion to the stimulus. This is, again, the lightning rod effect.

Height and Weight

Perhaps the major concern for boys is height, which is considered to be the most important index of manhood and attractiveness to women. Although the "tall, dark, and handsome" label does not fit all of today's leading men, it nonetheless remains an image to which many young men aspire. Among boys, the growth spurt of adolescence begins usually at about age twelve or thirteen (but can begin as early as age ten and a half or as late as age sixteen), is most rapid during the fourteenth year (when some boys can gain four to six inches in height), and ends at age sixteen (but can end as early as age thirteen and a half or as late as seventeen and a half). Some additional growth in height can occur until the twentieth year in boys, but by age sixteen most boys have attained some 98 percent of their total adult height.[11]

The boy who grows tall during this period is complimented by almost everyone: family friends remark on how tall he is getting. In addition, he feels taller emotionally. He can look down on his mother and sometimes on his father as well. More generally, being able to look down on people during conversation conveys a sense of power and control. It is for that reason, in part at least, that kings sat on thrones. Being tall can also bring problems (for girls as well as for boys). Tall teenagers may be treated according to how old they look rather than how old they are. And they can be teased unrelentingly by insensitive remarks like "How's the weather up there?" (Girls often hear, "Geez, the Amazons have arrived!") But in general in our society, the teenage boy who grows tall (5'9" or above) finds there are more positive than negative benefits associated with his height. This is not as true for girls, who may feel that undue height (above 5'7") limits their range of choices among young men. For whatever reason, young men prefer young women who are shorter or at least not taller than they are.

For boys who attain average or above-average height, the most dangerous peril of puberty has probably been passed successfully. But for boys not as fortunate, height may become the worst peril of puberty. When they express their concern over their height, they voice the same self-consciousness girls feel over their bodies. Listen to what one boy wrote about his height:

> I'm real short and everyone in my class thinks I'm nothing but a clown. It's true, I'm apt to come up with a fast remark and usually can make kids laugh, but sometimes I wish they would treat me like a real person, not just a joke.[12]

This boy has found a way to compensate for his small stature, but for the teen years he may well continue to be sensitive about his height. Parents have to be alert to these concerns. It may help to remind such young men that there are several short leading men, including Dudley Moore (5'3"), Dustin Hoffman (5'7"), and Paul Newman (5'8"), who appear to be quite attractive to large numbers of women. In the same way, height seems to be no barrier to creativity and fame, as is indicated by the success of William Faulkner (5'6") and John Cheever (5'5"). It is perhaps unnecessary to mention Napoleon (5'), who was no slouch in matters military.

Weight tends to be less of a problem for teenage boys than for teenage girls, but many boys are overweight largely because of poor eating habits. At least 30 percent of today's teenagers are overweight to some degree. But only when this overweight is more than 25 to 30 percent of total recommended weight is there a chance of serious health problems. Nonetheless, it is healthier for young people to maintain the appropriate weight for their height. Many teenage boys who were chubby as children become lean and slender as teenagers. Unfortunately, the reverse is also true.

Dr. Judith J. Wurtman of the Department of Nutrition of Massachusetts Institute of Technology has suggested ways in which parents can help teenagers control their weight:

> Parents should make it easy for teens and younger children to lose weight or prevent rapid weight gain by not buying or making calorie-dense foods, serving meals that are not excessively high in fat, and by not keeping the refrigerator stocked with foods that are high in calories. Also, if parents exercise routinely—biking, long walks, swimming, badminton in the back yard—their children will view exercise as a normal part of life. (Just don't make the walk an excuse to go to the local ice cream store!)[13]

Sexual Development

Changes in a boy's sexual apparatus begin between the ages of ten and thirteen and a half with the gradual enlargement of the testes. This enlargement continues for three or more years and can end anywhere from age fourteen and a half to age eighteen. Pubic hair begins to appear at about the same time as the enlargement of the testes. As the boy matures, pubic hair continues to spread in area and to become darker, coarser, and curlier. By maturity, the triangular pubic hair pattern so common in women is less clear in men, in whom pubic hair can become continuous with the hair on the chest and the abdomen.[14]

Of greatest concern to boys is the growth in the size of the penis. This organ grows rapidly about a year after the growth in the testes has begun and pubic hair has appeared, usually between the ages of ten and a half and thirteen and a half. This growth continues until ages thirteen and a half to sixteen and a half. The average penis size is between four and six inches in a flaccid state. Because there is so much wrong (and some-

55

times mythical) information about penis size, let me quote an authority on the subject:

> The size and the shape of the penis are not related to a man's physique, race, virility or ability to give or to receive pleasure. Like any organ, penises differ in size, but the differences tend to diminish in the erect state. The penis neither atrophies with lack of use nor enlarges through frequent use.[15]

For many teenagers this kind of accurate information can be extremely important in easing their fears and confusion. And even though adults attempt to make available accurate information about sexuality, the mythologies about the size of the sexual organs and sexual functions may persist. Consider this letter from a teenager:

> You may think I'm kidding but my penis is too big. It's nine inches in a relaxed state. The guys all call me names like Super Stud and worse, and they say that I will never be able to marry a normal woman. Is this true?[16]

By far the largest store of mythology about a boy's sexuality has to do with masturbation. An interchange that occurs between two boys when one finds the other in a toilet stall at school reflects several of the commonly held beliefs about the effects of masturbation. This kind of ignorance can be combated only with information and patience.

> "Hey, Jimmy, man you've been in there an awful long time. What are you doing?"
> How does he know I'm here? I look at the floor. My red sneakers gave me away. I should have stood on the seat. Too late now, so I answer him, real matter of fact, "I'm reading."
> "Yeh, sure you're reading," he chuckles. "I know what you're doing in there. Feeling good, huh? Come on now, you can tell old Tony boy."
> So that's what he thinks I'm doing. I hear him walking toward my stall.
> "You'd better watch out. If you do it too much, it's going

to fall off. They say you can grow hair on your palms. You know—leprosy. Ever hear of that? It's true.[17]

This kind of concern with masturbation and its effects has a long history. Consider this reminiscence from G. Stanley Hall, the "father" of adolescent psychology. Hall grew up during the middle of the nineteenth century, and his account gives us a sense of how young men thought about masturbation at that time.

> So great was my dread of natural phenomena that in the earliest moment I rigged an apparatus and applied bandages to prevent erethism while I slept which very likely augmented the trouble. If I yielded to any kind of experimentation on myself, I suffered intense remorse and fear and sent up many a secret and fervent prayer that I might never again break my resolve. At one time, I feared I was abnormal and found occasion to consult a physician in a neighboring town who did not know me. He examined me and took my dollar, and laughed at me, but also told me what consequences would ensue if I became unchaste. What an untold anguish of soul would have been saved me if some one had told me that certain experiences while I slept were normal for boys in their teens as are the monthly phenomena of girls.[18]

Despite the mythologies and taboos about masturbation, teenagers widely engage in the practice. A recent survey suggests that more than 75 percent of teenage boys masturbate and that 50 percent to 60 percent of girls do the same. Boys start masturbating earlier than girls, with 50 percent engaging in the practice by age thirteen. Only 37 percent of teenage girls are masturbating at that age. The frequency of masturbation varies with the teenager's age and sex. Boys masturbate more often than girls, and older boys (ages seventeen to eighteen) more often than younger boys (ages fifteen to sixteen). The majority of young people discover masturbation by themselves, and a majority of teenagers (70 percent) approve of masturbation.[19]

The issue of masturbation confronts the teenager with the

question of self-control, the control over impulses. The issue thus has broader implications, for it suggests to the teenager whether he or she will be able to control other impulses, such as those of overeating. If teenagers feel that they have mastered the impulse in one area, they feel more confident that they can master it in another area. Unfortunately, the reverse is also true: if the young person feels at the mercy of sexual impulses, he or she will feel overwhelmed by other impulses as well. Gaining a sense of control over one's impulses occurs gradually and involves struggle and effort, as Halls's recollection suggests. But such struggle is part of a positive form of growth and can contribute to a healthy sense of personal identity if, in the end, the young person feels in charge of his or her inner desires.

Another issue of control associated with a boy's sexual maturity is the unwanted erection. Once boys have experienced the spontaneous hardening of the penis and the resultant bulge in their pants, they become concerned about when and where this will happen. A common fantasy of this kind is the following fictional one from Judy Blume's *Then Again, Maybe I Won't:*

> This morning in math class, I wasn't thinking about Lisa. I was concentrating on a problem in my book. When I got the answer I raised my hand and Miss Tobin called on me. She asked me to go to the board and show the class how it worked out.
>
> Just as I finished writing the figures on the board, I started to get hard. Mind over matter . . . Mind over matter, I told myself. But still it went up. I kept my back to the class and prayed for it to go down.
>
> Miss Tobin said, "That's an interesting way to solve the problem, Tony."
>
> For a minute I thought she meant my real problem. But then I realized she was talking about the math problem.
>
> "Could you explain your reasoning to the class, Tony?"
>
> I started talking but I didn't turn around. I could just picture facing the class. Everybody would laugh and point at my pants. I wished I were wearing my raincoat.
>
> "We'd hear better if you'd turn around," Miss Tobin said.

> What could I do? Pretend to be sick and run out of the room? Maybe. Or just refuse to turn around? No. Ask to go to the bathroom? No . . .
>
> "Tony," Miss Tobin said.
>
> "Yes?"
>
> "We're waiting for you to explain the problem."
>
> "Oh, okay Miss Tobin."
>
> "I was holding my math book in my left hand and a piece of chalk in my right. I turned sideways, keeping my book in front of my pants. I explained my answer as fast as I could and Miss Tobin didn't ask me any questions. She said, "Thank you, Tony, you can sit down now."
>
> I walked back to my seat still holding the math book close to me. But I didn't have to worry. By then it was down.
>
> From now on I'm going to make sure I always have a stack of books with me. Books are a lot better than any old raincoat.[20]

This kind of incident is particularly embarrassing because of the belief in the imaginary audience, which leads the young person to feel that everybody in the room is aware of his condition.

The physical changes associated with puberty become perils precisely because teenagers have no way of knowing definitely how things will turn out. The teenage boy or girl will have to wait several years before he or she can feel secure in his or her body. The worries that plague teenagers are nevertheless healthy because they are symptoms of positive growth and bear witness to the teenager's concern with how much he or she is like or different from other young people. However stressful these worries are, they help the young person to attain a strong definition of self that will be a bulwark against stress at a later age. Before we go on to the more serious perils of puberty, here are some of the other worries of teenagers, amusingly presented by Delia Ephron in *Teenage Romance*:

> Worry that there is a right way to neck and you don't know it.
>
> Worry that your date will be able to tell that you don't know it.

If you are a girl, worry that your breasts are too round. Worry that your breasts are too pointed. Worry that your nipples are the wrong color. Worry that your breasts point in different directions.

If you are a boy, worry that you will get breasts.

Worry that your nose is too fat. Worry that your nose is too long. Worry that your neck is too fat. Worry that your lips are too fat. Worry that your ass is too fat. Worry that your ears stick out. Worry that your eyes are too close together.

If you are a boy, worry that you will never be able to grow a moustache.

If you are a girl, worry that you have a moustache.

Worry that you won't like the food at the other people's houses.

Worry that you will eat too much food at other people's houses.

Worry that when you go to the bathroom people will hear.

Worry that the lock on the door doesn't work and someone will come in.

Worry that everyone hates you.

Worry that everyone thinks you are stupid.

Worry that you have ugly toes.[21]

These are only some of the perils of puberty. With time most young people incorporate their various physical features into their sense of personal identity. And when these features are put in the context of the young person's other qualities— intelligence, loyalty, good humor, and so on—they come to play a much less prominent part in the young person's self-evaluation. So, even though the sensitivity and concern that teenagers experience so exquisitely are never lost entirely, they diminish as teenagers get older and construct a broader self-definition.

Homosexuality

So far we have talked about puberty as it is experienced by the majority of young people. But there is a smaller group, about one in ten young people, who experience a different kind of peril. Although it is true that most of us go through a brief phase when we are attracted to members of the same sex— usually in early adolescence—this is only in part sexual. It stems from admiration, perhaps even envy, of someone we wish to look, or be, like. But for some teenagers, this is not a temporary but rather a permanent attraction. There are many theories about the origins of homosexuality, but its universality suggests that it may, in part at least, be genetic. Many of the young people to whom I have talked about their homosexuality tell me that they knew they were gay even when they were children, but they did not realize the full meaning of their orientation until they reached adolescence.

The stigma of homosexuality is far less serious today than it was formerly (in 1983 a gay writer and actor won a Tony for Best Play and another for Best Actor and currently has another hit play, about homosexuals, on Broadway); nevertheless, it is still very difficult for parents to accept. Indeed, in my talks with homosexual teenagers, I found that the hardest part for them was not in accepting their own homosexuality but rather in telling their parents. The following personal reflections by teenage homosexuals will help convey the pain of this particular peril of puberty:

> I'm a senior at St. Scholastica High School in Chicago. I'm seventeen years old and I am gay. Being gay is something I never really thought about until I was thirteen. All along I had had feelings for women, but I never really put a name to it.
>
> I was thirteen and a freshman when I met my first lover, Carla. Before we were lovers we were really close friends. After a few months, the relationship began to get physical. It was about then that I thought seriously about being gay. It wasn't until my sophomore year that I finally decided for sure that I was gay.
>
> Socially, both my parents and classmates expected me to date. I had a few boyfriends who were straight, but I knew one or two gay guys and we covered for each other.
>
> Being gay at an all-girl Catholic School is really hard. It

is even harder when your lover goes to school with you and you can't do anything, because the slightest sign of affection labels you for four years of school. Because Carla and I were so close, many people at school immediately guessed. That was really hard because people can be cruel when they don't understand. Some people just didn't talk to us. It got easier after Carla and I broke up junior year, because then I started dating people outside of school.[22]

My name is Mike Friedman, and I would like to relate a few of the experiences that I have had over the last few months because I think they may be of use to people who are in the same position. Last summer I finally came to grips with the fact that I was gay. I had been having sex with a man since I was fourteen but thought it was just a phase that I was going through. I thought that I would grow out of it, but obviously I didn't. Last summer I decided that I should stop kidding myself. I was gay, and I should be happy with the way I am.[23]

It is devastating, for some parents at least, to discover that their son or daughter is gay. No rationalization or philosophy can ease the pain. But as the preceding comments make clear, being gay is not something that the teenager is doing to hurt the parents, nor is it in any way the parents' fault. Freud was very clear in stating that homosexuality was not an illness or a sexual perversion but rather a different sexual orientation. What has to be remembered is that the vast majority of gay people are responsible, productive members of society whose sexual preference is a matter of their private, not their public, life.

The experience of gay young people reveals in sharp focus the struggle for self-definition that all teenagers must go through. All teenagers must come to accept some features of themselves that may not be attractive or socially acceptable or that fail to meet with the full approval of their parents. But coming to grips with who and what they are is part of constructive, positive growth. However painful it may be in the short run, in the long run the difficult process of growth by differentiation and integration provides the young person with a healthy sense of self that will mean a better future and a happier one.

Incest

Of all the perils of puberty, incest or its mere possibility is perhaps the most destructive. For most young people, gradually breaking away from parents and finding new love relations is a painful yet necessary step in the process of self-definition. But in some cases this process of breaking away and self-definition is made difficult and extraordinarily stressful when the teenager has been the object of sexual advances by another family member. In most cases this kind of experience involves a father or stepfather and teenage daughters. Less frequently incest involves brothers and sisters or stepbrothers and stepsisters. One consequence of the increased number of "blended" families today is probably a proportionate increase in this type of incest. Although figures are hard to come by, it has been estimated that approximately one million children and teenagers are sexually abused each year and that at least half this number have had an incestuous relationship.

Incestuous families are found in all socioeconomic strata and all ethnic groups. Although the specific dynamics vary from family to family, the most basic pattern is probably the Oedipal conflict described by Freud.[24] According to Freud, the preschool boy loves his mother and sees the father as a rival for her affections. Similarly, the girl loves the father and sees the mother as a rival (the Electra complex). Ordinarily these complexes are temporarily resolved as children move into childhood proper (ages six to ten).

> The significance of the Oedipal Complex as the central phenomenon of the sexual period of early childhood reveals itself more and more. After this disappears, it succumbs to repression, as we say, and is followed by the latency period. . . . Even when no special events . . . occur, the absence of the hoped for gratification, the continual frustration

of a wish for a child, causes the love lorn one to turn from its hopeless longing. According to this, the Oedipus complex becomes extinguished by its lack of success, the result of its inherent impossibility.[25]

During the latency period (childhood proper), the Oedipus complex lies dormant. But with the advent of puberty, the reawakening of sexual strivings, and the now-mature capacity for procreation, the Oedipal conflict is reawakened in a new and more powerful way.

> In analyzing adolescents, we investigate their repudiation of instinct. It is true that here, too, the starting point of the conflict is to be found in those centres of instinctual life which are subject to special prohibition, e.g., the incest-phantasies of the pre-pubertal period or the increased tendency to physical onanistic activities in which such wishes have their discharge.[26]

For the majority of teenagers the culmination of the Oedipal wish, although possible in a physical sense, is impossible psychologically. Most teenagers have internalized incest taboos and values that would prevent any sexual thoughts about the parent or at the very least make them extremely guilt- and anxiety-provoking. The same is true for the parent in whom the teenager evokes reciprocal attractions.

Nonetheless, remnants of the Oedipal conflict remain and can be seen in some familiar phenomena. Teenage girls, to illustrate, usually fight more with their mothers than with their fathers, whereas the reverse is likely to be true for teenage boys. In the same way, mothers may dote on their teenage sons, sometimes encouraging them to be what they would have liked their husbands to be. And fathers may take great pleasure in a teenage daughter's affection and can resent the boys she dates.

But in some families the normal restraints against incest have not been built in or do not function, and the Oedipal relationship occurs. Unlike rape, usually a one-time occurrence, incest may go on for months or even years. Some researchers suggest that much incest occurs with the tacit consent of the mother and that the arrangement may satisfy perverse needs in all members of the family. It is usually when the teenage girl starts forming new relationships that the whole story comes out and the pattern of relationships within the family is disrupted.

Several different patterns of incest or near-incest have been reported. In one pattern the father is introverted and nurturing and appears to be dependent:

> An example . . . [is] a man who complained to his daughter that her mother constantly left him to visit her own mother. The mother relied on this daughter, reversed roles and placed her in the parent role, forcing her to do much of the caring for younger siblings, cooking and housecleaning. Both father and daughter, missing mothering, turned to each other for an affectionate response that eventually became sexualized. Father said that he was concerned about the rest of his children and helped his daughter as she cared for them. At first he spent many hours talking to her and eventually they began to have intercourse.[27]

A very different pattern is exhibited by men who are hostile and aggressive. One man in particular

> terrorized his family with aggression. Owning a gun collection, at times he would shoot over the heads of various family members. The mother was passive, sickly, unavailable and had long since retreated from the scene. Much of the responsibility fell on the older daughters, and soon father had sexual relations with the two of them. He did not use overt aggression to force the relationship, but they became emotionally attached and dependent upon him. In an interview with one of the daughters, after she had become impregnated by her father, now in jail, she could barely talk. A very bright high school senior she could only say, between sobs, "I want my Daddy."[28]

Although some authorities argue that incest need not have lasting effects upon teenage girls, other studies strongly suggest that incest does have lifelong repercussions. The most commonly reported outcome of incestuous experiences is sexual acting out and promiscuity. Other young people who have had incestuous experiences may become homosexual as an expression of their extreme emotional pain and confusion. In addition, if and when incest is discovered, the teenage girl must suffer the guilt of being responsible for the father's (or other male's) punishment and for the disruption of the family. In general incest is only a symptom of a more pervasive family problem that can have a significant impact upon a young woman's emotional adjustment. One example of the impact incest can have on a young woman is revealed in the following recollection of a teenage girl's reaction to her stepfather's attempted incest.

> He used to wake me up for school. One morning, the last day of exams, he got into bed. I woke up and he was trying to get on top of me. I've never been so scared in my life. I didn't know what to do. He was totally nude, and trying to have sex with his wife's thirteen-year-old daughter!
>
> I got away from him and I screamed for him to get out of the room. He left without saying a word.
>
> That was the day I moved out, for good. I moved in with my father.
>
> I still can't look at my mother's husband without contempt and without wanting to smash his face into a thousand pieces. I still have massive hostility in me against him and my mother.[29]

Incest, like homosexuality, is an indication of the enormity of stress that teenagers may encounter even when the contemporary society is stable. Unlike homosexuality, however, which has become more socially acceptable, incest is a terrifying prospect. It is not something teenagers want to share with their friends, or with anyone, for that matter. Like rape, incest is a barrier to discovering the self, for it embeds in the person a sense of being vulnerable, of not really being in charge of the only thing we really have charge of, namely, our bodies. Once we understand the pain of incest, we can understand also why some young people want to adopt a ready-made substitute identity, such as those provided by cults.

Puberty brings with it a host of worries and anxieties, some of which are serious, others less so. These worries are symptoms of a constructive form of growth and are therefore healthy in the long run, even though they may be painful in the short run. Even in times of social stability, the stresses associated with the perils of puberty are considerable. They are clear evidence of teenagers' need for a special place and a protected time in society in order to cope with the transformations of their bodies and the social consequences those transformations entail.

Chapter 4

Peer Shock

S hock occurs when we are confronted with something both unexpected and apparently unmanageable. The sudden exposure to new ways of thinking and behaving that are at total variance with what we are accustomed to is often experienced as shock, as sudden and overwhelming stress. If a person moves abroad for business or professional reasons, for instance, the experience of a new culture can be a shock. People in a foreign country speak a different language and have different codes of behavior. Things are done differently. In restaurants in Switzerland, for example, even strangers greet you warmly; but on the street, people you work with do not greet you at all. Another, more trivial example of difference is that the Swiss pay their utility bills at the post office. Many such differences combined can produce severe stress for a foreigner living in Switzerland.

In many respects moving from the culture of childhood to the culture of adolescence is like moving from one society to another; and the change in behavior and conduct the adolescent encounters can lead to a form of shock—peer shock. The adolescent, expecting one form of behavior on the basis of past experience, is confronted with acts entirely unanticipated and must struggle to grasp the changes in his or her social world.

First of all, the structure of social relationships is different. Children come together mainly in play groups, and friendships are often determined mainly by who lives nearby. Who gets to play or not to play often depends upon who gets there first or who has the toys or the equipment. Among teenagers, however, belonging to a group is determined by such qualities as social status and ethnic background. As a consequence, many children who felt accepted by their peers as children suddenly experience, as young teenagers, the full impact of social prejudice. This is one type of peer shock, the shock of *exclusion*.

Second, social interaction among teenagers is different from that among children. When children socialize, their interactions are generally cooperative and centered on a common activity. Among teenagers social intercourse is much more complex and multilayered. Friendships are based on mutual trust and loyalty as well as upon the cooperation that dominates friendships in childhood. Because young people are still relatively inexperienced in these complex relationships, however, they often get hurt. They discover that their trust or their loyalty or their generosity was not reciprocated but rather used and exploited. Teenagers therefore experience a second type of peer shock, namely, the shock of *betrayal*.

It is not just the experiences of exclusion and betrayal that come as a shock to children moving into adolescence. There is another stressful experience that grows out of teenagers' new attraction for members of the opposite sex. Children, as we have seen, are generally in what Freud called the latency period, when the sexual drive is relatively quiescent. But with puberty the sexual drive emerges with full potency, and boys and girls, who tend to hold the opposite sex in contempt during childhood proper, suddenly find members of the opposite sex interesting to look at and to talk about. This is often more of an abrupt turnaround for boys than it is for girls, who tend to be more socially oriented and more attuned to what is coming. With their new capacity for idealization, young people form "crushes" on other teenagers who seem perfect in every way. But these crushes are short-lived, because they are projected onto mere humans. The discovery that the loved one has clay feet leads to the third form of peer shock, the shock of *disillusion*.

Adapting to the culture of adolescence thus presents the

teenager with many stresses. Yet, like the stresses associated with thinking in a new key and the perils of puberty, the various kinds of peer shock can be healthy if they contribute to the development of a strong identity and sense of self. Here again, the short-term shocks of adjustment can purchase long-term insurance against the stresses of adult life.

Fads, Clubs, and Cliques: The Shock of Exclusion

The broadest social grouping among teenagers is that of the fad: youngsters in different parts of the country and from different walks of life are joined together by participating in a fad of clothing or language or some other item in their lives. Participation in fads defines the adolescent as someone who is different from both children and adults, albeit at a highly superficial level. Participation in fads also amounts to a kind of growth by substitution, an attempt to give the impression of inner transformation by means of outer alterations. But true, constructive growth, growth by differentiation and integration, does not come about as easily as modifying language or wearing new clothing styles.

As an example of such teenage fads (which quickly become passé, as this one has) we can look at the recent Val Gal phenomenon. It is a phenomenon, that is, a variation on a familiar theme. It is merely a contemporary rendition of what in earlier generations were called flappers or bobby-soxers or teeny boppers.

> All of a sudden, from Tarzana, California, to Tarrytown, New York, everyone with a teenage daughter was wondering: "Is she one?" A Valley Girl, that is. If she was from a fairly well-to-do family and between the ages of thirteen and seventeen, chances are she was. If her passions were shopping, popularity, pigging out on junk food, and piling on cosmetics, the answer was probably, "Fer shurr." If her speech was almost unintelligible, the verdict could only be, "Totally." Particularly if she pronounced the word "toe-dully."[1]

Participation in fads usually occurs in early adolescence.

The adolescent culture is a complex one, and many young people get their feet wet, so to speak, by participating in a fad that is shared almost exclusively by teenagers. Boys tend not to go to the same extremes as girls, but they, too, get caught up with the fads of clothing that are dictated by their age group. Fads open the door for an adolescent, but the real struggle for acceptance into adolescent society revolves around clubs and cliques. Exclusion from fads is much more a matter of money and taste than of personal qualities. Nonetheless, for some young people who cannot participate in the fad, the momentary exclusion can be most painful.

Clubs tend to be formed by groups of teenagers who share some aspects of their lives. Teenagers who share the same social class, ethnic background, and intellectual level tend to want to make this relationship public by the formation of a club with its own name, dues, president, initiation rites, and so on. These clubs provide a good example of a kind of social differentiation that parallels the teenagers' personal efforts along the same lines. Teenagers who are members of the club emphasize their likenesses to one another; by excluding others from membership, they can emphasize their differences.

Clubs or groups often arrange themselves into hierarchies of social status and in this way provide the teenager with still another piece of information for his or her self-definition. Here is a writer's memory of the club arrangements when she was growing up:

> If I couldn't be a member of the Society Six, I was delighted to be accepted into the next group on the social scale, a larger, more fluid one, ten or fifteen girls, democratic enough at least to be nameless. . . . The other girls in this group were from various backgrounds, some with faculty parents, others with fathers who included an insurance salesman, a banker, a plumber, an oil company representative who toured the state for Mobil. What your father did wasn't important, though you needed to have a house where you could bring friends home without embarrassment.
>
> Most of us attended the nearby Presbyterian, Methodist,

or Baptist churches, but by ninth grade, when parochial schools ended, we had two Catholic friends, as well. I'm not sure on what grounds we admitted others as friends, how we made up the guest lists for our slumber parties or Valentines or birthdays, or how we knew whom to call to go to the movies. Most of us went on to college, but we certainly didn't base our friendship on intellectual merit. Most of us were moderately attractive, but one or two of us didn't date at all for years. Most of us were "popular," but I don't know exactly why. Perhaps we just defined ourselves in relation to the Society Six and to all the other girls below us, the loners, the stupid ones, the fat ones. We had absorbed by sixth grade a set of careful and cruel distinctions.[2]

The "careful and cruel distinctions" amount to rules of exclusion that can come as a devastating shock to young people who never thought of themselves as different before. Exclusion is hurtful because it forces us to acknowledge that other people may not see us the way we see ourselves. The shock of exclusion is thus a painful but necessary process by which we attain a more realistic view of how we are seen by others.

The last and most intimate type of grouping is the clique. This is often a small group of young people who do almost everything together. Although cliques tend to be very exclusive, the members sometimes change. This usually happens when the clique has three members. Three is a bad number sociologically because inevitably there is a choosing of sides, which ultimately means there are two against one. This happens in families of three children, in dormitories where three students are assigned to a single room, and to groups of friends who "hang out" together. Because of the intensity of the relationships, cliques provide the most telling learning experiences. Although the twelve-year-old heroine of Carson McCullers's *A Member of the Wedding* is not a member of a clique, she does want to become a member of the wedding couple:

> She wanted to speak to her brother and the bride, to talk to them and tell them of her plans, the three of them alone together, but they were never once alone; Jarvis was out

73

checking the car someone was lending for the honeymoon while Janice dressed in the front bedroom among a crowd of beautiful grown girls. She wandered from one to the other of them, unable to explain. And once Janice put her arms about her, and said she was so glad to have a little sister—and when Janice kissed her, F. Jasmine felt an aching in her throat and could not speak. Jarvis, when she went to find him in the yard, lifted her up in a roughhouse way and said: Frankie the lankie the alaga fankie, the tee-legged, toe-legged, bow-legged Frankie. And he gave her a dollar.

    She stood in the corner of the bride's room, wanted to say: I love the two of you so much and you are the "we of me." Please take me with you from the wedding, for we belong together.[3]

The longing of F. Jasmine (Frankie) to be a part of the relationship between her brother and his wife, her discovery of her need to be a part of a group—"the we of me"—speaks eloquently of adolescents' discovery of their need to belong to a peer group as well as the anguish of exclusion.

Strategic Manipulation: The Shock of Betrayal

We engage in strategic interactions whenever we try to withhold, obtain, or provide information in order to win some personal advantage.[4] Perhaps the most straightforward example occurs when players in a poker game attempt to maintain a poker face. Each player tries not to reveal by facial expression how good or bad a hand he or she has. Clearly the maintenance of a neutral expression is much to the player's advantage. If you have a straight flush and you grin widely at the other players, everyone is going to drop out; the bidding will end quickly and the pot will be small. Of course, some players may "bluff" by pretending to have a good hand when in fact they do not have one.

    Part of the game of poker is strategic and revolves around the player's skill at strategic interactions. Such interactions clearly require formal operational thinking. To engage in that sort of strategic interaction, you have to be able to think about the other person's thinking, and that comes with thinking in a new key. Teenagers are capable of engaging in strategic interactions but are inexperienced in knowing when such interactions are in play. In obvious instances like poker and competitive team sports, it is clear to teenagers and others that everyone is engaged in strategic interactions. Everyone knows, for example, that the quarterback will communicate the upcoming play to his teammates by means of a secret numerical code.

In our day-to-day interactions we are usually not strategic. If someone asks how we are, we take them at their word and say, "Fine, thank you. How are you?" If someone asks us for the time, we generally comply if we have it. Nonstrategic behavior is based on cooperation and a willingness to withhold, provide, or conceal information for the benefit of others. Friendship, to illustrate, is a nonstrategic, or *frame*, interaction.[5] Friendship means sharing information that will be useful or beneficial to one's friend. The information itself can be positive (a stock tip) or negative (what someone is saying behind your back), but it is shared because it is perceived as useful to the other person. At other times a friend may withhold information (information that would be painful without being constructive) or obtain information (what one person thinks about another) for the other person's benefit.

It is a very different situation when one or more persons are being strategic and those interacting with them are not. This is the basis for strategic *manipulation*. The famous "sting" of the con artist is an example. Stings take place when one party is operating on a cooperative frame basis while the other is being strategic. Consider an elderly person who is befriended by a con artist. The elderly person may behave according to the normal standards of friendship and reveal his or her financial status, as one might to a friend. The con artist might then talk about an investment—apparently sharing information on the basis of friendship—that is sure to double the money invested in the next couple of years. The elderly person, still assuming that the other person is acting according to the dictates of a cooperative frame relationship, accepts that information as valid and proceeds to act upon it by giving the con artist money to invest. This is a "sting," or manipulation. When we are operating strategically, we are forewarned to distrust the information provided by the other person. But when we are operating in a frame defined by the rules of friendship or proper conduct, we are predisposed to accept the information provided by the other person as true.

Here is another, less hurtful example. A girl who has run away from home sees her picture in the newspaper. The paper is being read by a woman who has taken her in, befriended her, and given her a job. Rather than deny that the picture is of her, this is how the girl handles the situation strategically:

> Once I picked up the paper and looked hard at the picture. "Do you think she looks like me?" I asked Mrs. Peacock, and Mrs. Peacock leaned back and looked at me and then at the picture and then at me again and finally she shook her head and said, "No, if you wore your hair longer and curlier, and your face was maybe a little fuller, there might be a little resemblance, but then if you looked like a homicidal maniac I wouldn't ever let you in my house."
>
> "I kinda think she looks like me," I said.
>
> "You get along to work and stop being vain," Mrs. Peacock said.[6]

In this instance the teenager gives out information as a way of concealing it. Mrs. Peacock responds accordingly to the rules of friendship; she does not doubt the honesty of her young friend.

Strategic manipulations are also what teenagers employ when they steal. In so doing, of course, they violate relationships that are based on the honest sharing of information. When we buy something at a store, we reveal to the clerk all of the items we wish to purchase; we are behaving according to certain frame rules. But if we conceal one or all of the items we wish to take out of the store, we are engaging in a strategic manipulation: we are concealing information for our own benefit and to the detriment of others. Many teenagers who are raised to believe that people engage in strategic interactions only when everyone involved is alerted to that fact are shocked to discover that some teenagers engage in strategic manipulation. They experience this as a kind of betrayal.

> One afternoon I needed some notebook paper so I stopped into the corner store next to Ben's Sweet Shop. Joel was with me. I decided as long as I was in the store, I needed a new ball point pen, too. My old one leaks on my fingers and smudges a lot. The pens were displayed in a mug, practically in front of the cash register. While I was deciding what color pen to buy, Joel picked two out of the mug and put them in his pocket. I think he took one ball point and one felt tip. They cost 49 cents. Joel didn't look at me. He just smiled his crooked smile and hummed a little tune.
>
> I was furious, just furious. I wanted to punch Joel in the nose. I wanted to mess up his angel face, to see the blood ooze out of his nostrils and trickle down his chin. I wanted to look him in the eye and say "I've had it with you, Joel! You stink!"[7]

The narrator was betrayed by a friend who not only violated the rules of conduct followed by honest people in a store but also imposed that violation on the narrator by making him a witness to that act. This was a double betrayal and an experience that undoubtedly helped one narrator recognize certain traits of honesty in himself.

The shock of betrayal comes in many different forms, but in every case the teenager discovers that while he or she was operating according to one set of frame rules, the free and honest sharing of information, the other person was operating strategically, obtaining, concealing, or conveying information for personal advantage. Another example of the shock of betrayal encountered by teenagers occurs when they are led on by someone of the opposite sex. Here again, one person is operating strategically, giving out information for his or her own benefit when the other person assumes that other rules are being followed, that the information provided is honest and given for his or her benefit. In the following fictional account from a short story by A. Muro entitled "Cecilia Rosas," a young man takes a woman's overtures seriously, only to find later that they were meant for her amusement and that of her friends:

> "Amadito," she whispered the way I had always dreamed she would.
>
> "Yes, Señorita Cecilia," I said expectantly.
>
> Her smile was warmly intimate. "Amadito, when are you going to take me to the movies?" she asked.
>
> Other salesladies watched us. They made me so nervous I couldn't answer.
>
> "Amadito, you haven't answered me," Miss Rosas said teasingly. "Either you are as bashful as a village sweetheart, or else you don't like me at all." . . .
>
> "Señorita Cecilia," I said, "I would love to take you to the movies any time."
>
> Miss Rosas smiled and patted my cheek, "Will you buy me candy and popcorn?" she said.
>
> I nodded, putting my hand on the warm imprint her warm palm had left on my face.
>
> "And hold my hand?"
>
> I said "yes" so enthusiastically it made her laugh. Other salesladies laughed too. Dazed and numb with happiness, I watched Miss Rosas walk away.

Later, when Amado prepares to serenade Miss Rosas, he meets her as she is leaving with another man:

> "Ay Amado, you're going to serenade your girl," she said. I didn't reply right away. Then when I was getting ready to say "Señorita Cecilia, I came to serenade you," I saw the American man sitting in the sports roadster at the curb.
>
> Miss Rosas turned to him. "I'll be right there, Johnny," she said. "Have a nice time, darling."
>
> I looked at her silken legs as she got into the car. Everything had happened so fast I was dazed. Broken dreams made my head spin. The contrast between myself and the poised American in the sports roadster was so cruel it made me wince.[8]

Although Miss Rosas and the other salesladies may have assumed that Amado knew that Miss Rosas was teasing (being strategic), he did not and experienced the shock of betrayal. The experience leaves him sadder but wiser. As he himself states, he was clearly different from the man she preferred and became painfully aware of another part of himself. Here is how the incident ends:

> Just about then Miss Rosas' father looked up from his newspaper. He asked the mariachis [whom Amado had hired to help him serenade Miss Rosas] if they knew how to sing Canena Jail. They told him they did. Then they looked at me. I thought it over for a moment, then I nodded and started strumming the bass strings of my guitar. What had happened made it only too plain I could never trust Miss Rosas again. So we serenaded her father instead.[9]

Amado may have been embarrassed, betrayed, injured, but he ultimately accepted what he saw of himself through Miss Rosas's behavior and took another step toward understanding and accepting who he was.

Another common strategic manipulation involves the girl who is operating according to the frame rules for romance. In this type of relationship both parties are supposed to share honestly their feelings of attraction and admiration for each other. But if the boy is operating strategically, giving and withholding information for his own benefit, the result is strategic manipulation, and the girl ends up experiencing the shock of exploitation.

> I had intercourse twice even though I didn't want to. I was madly in love with this guy and he and his friend picked me up one night in their car and we drove around. Suddenly, he just stopped the car and told me that if I ever wanted to see him again, I'd have to have sex right now with him and his friend. I loved him so much and didn't want to lose him so I did it. God, I hated myself afterward. I don't see him anymore and I'll never have sex with anyone unless I want to. Sex isn't a toy. It should be something very special.[10]

In this all-too-common experience of exploitation, we see how teenagers can abuse the capacity for strategic interaction. But again, through her painful experience, this girl has learned about herself and her identity.

Perhaps it is wise to say at this point, too, that not all teenage behavior can be explained away or excused by social pressure, stress, and the like. We have to assume that at least some modicum of human decency is inborn and that, to a certain degree, the teenager must be held responsible for his or her own behavior. It would be wrong, a serious mistake, I believe, to excuse any and all teenage misbehavior as a consequence of bad upbringing and social upheaval. These factors are important, particularly today, but at some point teenagers must be held accountable for their own actions. Teenagers are under more stress today than ever before, and they have fewer resources for coping than earlier generations had. But even these circumstances cannot excuse any and all actions. *This book is not an apology or an excuse for brutish behavior on the part of young people*.

Once teenagers become aware of strategic manipulation, they may become suspicious of other people's motives. This usually occurs in later adolescence, after they have had one or more experiences of betrayal. Sometimes, however, they can suspect a betrayal when it is not in fact intended. This was the tragic circumstance described by John Knowles in his classic novel, *A Separate Peace*:

> I believed him, the joking manner was a screen; I believed him. In front of my eyes the trigonometry textbook blurred into a jumble. I couldn't see. My brain exploded. He minded, despised the possibility that I might be the head of the school. There was a swift chain of explosions in my brain one certainty after another blasted up like a detonation. Up went the idea of my best friend, up went affection and partnership and sticking by someone and relying on someone absolutely in the jungle of a boys' school, up went the hope that there was anyone in this school—in this world—whom I could trust.''[11]

The shock of betrayal can come in many different forms and varieties. However painful, these experiences can help young people to be more discriminating and to discern when people are being strategic under the guise of friendship. Moreover, they contribute to a clearer perception of the self, because they teach young people how they are vulnerable to manipulation.

Romantic Attachments: The Shock of Disillusion

Young people are romantic; they fall in love with love. Thinking in a new key allows them to think of love in an idealistic and hence romantic way. They see only the good of romance, and if there is a struggle to win the girl or boy of their dreams, they can nonetheless be sure that they will "live happily ever after." In accord with this romantic inclination, young people tend to idealize both the people they admire and the young people to whom they are romantically attracted. Inevitably these idealizations have to be modified by experience, and this leads to a third form of peer shock, the shock of disillusion.

One form of disillusion occurs when someone we admire expresses admiration for someone we dislike. Teenagers, for example, often admire an older brother or sister whom they look up to and would like to emulate. It often comes as a shock to these young teenagers to discover the sort of person the admired sibling is attracted to. Listen to this girl describe her moment of disillusionment with her older brother:

> My brother the basketball player invited his new girl-friend to a family dinner not long ago. My brother is terribly quiet, shy, and so very tall you wouldn't believe me if I told you his height. His girlfriend, on the other hand, looks like a plump littly gypsy, with jet black curls and bangles up and down her chubby little arms. She barely comes up to his waist and from the moment she arrived she never shut up. She babbled and babbled and the next morning my mother groused,

"What is he doing with her? What is this thing your brother has for short chatterboxes."[12]

Another, reverse kind of disillusion occurs when we discover that someone we like or are attracted to does not have the same effect upon other people whose opinion we value. When young people make a romantic choice, they expect others to see in the person what they see in him or her. This is often not the case, and it comes as a shock to many teenagers to discover that others do not like the choice they have made, as one writer explains:

> Regardless of the kind of guy you prefer, someone is bound to find fault with your selection. Friends and family members often have their own ideas about who is right for you. And peer and parental pressures often can make it difficult to date a boy who doesn't meet everyone's idea of Mr. Right.[13]

An illustration of this situation is provided by the fictional romances popular among teenagers today. In one story, the heroine, Lauren, has been dating dashing Brad during the summer, but as fall draws near and she prepares to return home, she must decide whether to pursue her romance with Brad or return to her less dashing but steadier boyfriend back home, Randy. In the following passages she describes the conflict between her personal feelings and evaluations of her friends and mother:

> The past few weeks with Brad had been a little strange. Sometimes I thought I really liked him and sometimes I wasn't so sure. I'd spent a lot of time thinking about the things Kim and Ellen had said, that Brad was kind of conceited and would forget all about me when he went back to college. Mom hadn't said anything lately, but I just knew she wasn't really thrilled about him.
> Long before the tournament even Elizabeth had said she

liked Randy better. Okay, so maybe they were right in some ways, I thought, but still, they had to see that Brad was gorgeous and a fantastic tennis player. Maybe he did think he was a little too cool and maybe he did have a girlfriend back home and maybe he did drink a little bit, but so what. Leaving Brad wasn't going to be easy, no matter what everybody else thought about him.[14]

Although the discovery that other people do not share your opinion of someone you are infatuated with can be hard to take, it can be healthy. Love may be blind, but sometimes friends and parents can help to restore our vision. It is part of the slow process of learning that the way things are is not always the way we would like them to be. Lauren's thoughts as she tries to justify Brad's character give a hint of the push-and-pull that occurs when we choose someone whom others consider bad for us.

Even more disillusioning is the discovery that someone to whom you are romantically attached does not share the same standards and values. According to one writer, Don Weir, "Most boys believe that girls really do respond to the macho type, and some girls give them little reason to believe otherwise. There is nothing more devastating for a shy, sensitive teenage boy than the sight of a girl he has a crush on mooning over some superficial jerk."[15] In the same way, there is nothing so disillusioning to a sensitive, intelligent young woman than the sight of the boy she feels attracted to going "ape" over some well-endowed but empty-headed girl. Nonetheless, these shocks of disillusion can be useful learning experiences in helping young people to differentiate between physical attraction and personal compatibility.

There are other shocks of disillusion for young people as they begin to date and "get physical." "Getting physical" can be quite disenchanting, particularly if one person has greatly overidealized the other. What follows is a fictional passage about a young teenager who has fantasized all winter about a lifeguard she has known on summer vacations for many summers past.

And above all Jim, sitting in his high chair, watching and making the world small and safe. . . . When Jim comes, Nancy thought, then it will be all right, when Jim comes.

When summer arrives, the family moves to the shore and Nancy finally encounters Jim at the beach:

> She was sharply aware of the slight pressure of his hand on her arm, of the naked upper half of his body so close to her own. "Don't you work any?" Her breath was coming in hard little gasps. "I mean don't you have a regular kind of job?"
>
> "Don't need to," he said. "Got enough to eat on. Got a little shack up there, back a way. It's a good enough little place. I'll show it to you one day, if you like."
>
> "No," she said nervously. "I mean, Mother wouldn't let me."
>
> "Mother wouldn't let me," he mimicked, and his teeth glistened whitely against the brown of his skin. "What a baby you are, Nancy."
>
> He was squeezing her arm. Glancing sideways, she watched a fat pink worm of a tongue crawl from between his lips. She stood motionless an instant. Then, shaking her head frantically, she jerked away from his hand and darted forward. She lifted her feet high, running, with the water splashing against her legs, pushed forward against an oncoming breaker, half fell, and stood again, holding the thick wet rope with one hand.
>
> Looking back, she could see the beach, the mothers on their blankets, the children playing in the sand. Off to the left was her own mother, with the tiny blond girl, very close, still digging. She watched Jim climb to the top of his stand and sit, brown and still and watchful. It was for this that she had waited, all through the winter. She turned away, and the ocean stretched vast and terrifying before her. "Mother," she said. And her lips sought and found an earlier name. "Mama, mama." She hesitated briefly, her eyes burning with unshed tears. Taking a deep breath, she ducked under the rope that marked off the outermost limit for children.[16]

As Nancy's experience illustrates, physical encounters are often not the romantic "ringing of bells" they are reputed to be. In reality, the shock of disillusion can be so painful that the teenager may wish to return to childhood, where "getting physical" does not have to be dealt with and one is protected by one's parents. Again, however, such painful disillusionment can be constructive in helping the young person differentiate between the ideal and the real. And each new discovery about others always occasions a new discovery about oneself that can eventually be incorporated into a healthy identity and definition of oneself.

The event that teenagers fantasize about the most is "doing it"—losing their virginity. Studies suggest that teenagers, particularly girls, move gradually toward greater sexual intimacies—heavy petting and intercourse—through a series of dating and going-steady experiences. Rates of nonmarital petting have increased over the past fifty years, particularly for girls and for young adolescents.[17] Several decades ago, there was a gap between the percentage of teenage girls who engaged in "heavy petting" and those who engaged in sexual intercourse. Kinsey reported that about 84 percent of the females in his study were petting by age eighteen but only 10 percent were having intercourse. Studies conducted more recently indicate that the gap has narrowed dramatically since Kinsey's work in the early 1950s. In 1979, 48.5 percent of senior high school girls and 53 percent of senior boys were not virgins. Still more recent figures indicate that the percentage of teenage boys and girls who are sexually active has continued to increase at a fast pace.

Boys and girls view the loss of virginity quite differently, and the kind of disillusion they may experience is therefore also different. Basically boys are more erotic and girls more romantic. Whether the reason is biological, psychological, or sociological, or some combination of the three, boys have a different sexual orientation from that of girls. For example, in a recent survey of teenagers, about 50 percent of the boys said that they would want to have intercourse with a girl after going out with her for a month or less. Only 13 percent of the girls felt this way. On the other hand, 53 percent of the girls said they would have intercourse with a boy only if in love with him; only about 30 percent of the boys felt love was a prerequisite.[18]

Not surprisingly, the fantasies that boys and girls have about intercourse are quite different. Girls tend to think about it as part of a romantic, loving relationship. At the same time they worry that if they go "all the way," they will lose their reputation. They are also concerned that if they do agree to intercourse, the boy will not respect them any longer and will not, to use an old-fashioned expression, "stay for breakfast." Boys, on the other hand, think much less about the partner than they do about the act itself, which becomes something like a rite of passage, an important step toward adulthood. Obviously, there are wide individual differences; some boys are more romantic than girls and some girls are only out for a good time. But for the majority of teenagers, the portrayal given above is roughly accurate.

The difference between the boy's and the girl's viewpoint on this matter is amusingly but realistically portrayed in *Teenage Romance* by Delia Ephron. The following is an account of the simultaneous thoughts of two teenagers out on a date together:

> *Boy:* You bet you do, you know it, you're going to get it. Hey, hey, hey, tonight's the night, you feel it in your bones. Bones? Not bad! That's where you feel it all right. Or, should you say, bone! Check out your reflection in the glass of the ticket booth. Then on the way to join date at the end of the ticket holders' line see if you know anyone the two of you could butt in front of, and call yourself an asshole, if you don't stop thinking about getting it, you'll jinx it. Stop thinking, I know it, I'm going to get it, and consider instead what you could say to your date that would really help you get it for sure like a compliment. As soon as you see her ask her if she did something to her hair, it looks different.
>
> *Girl:* You know, you two really are a lot alike, it's amazing, it really is. Do you think he really likes you? Suppose he does. Think. Please God make him like me, make him like me really a lot. I really want him to. What if he said he loved you?

Imagine it, he falls in love with you. Then imagine telling your best friend all about the date tomorrow. Oh God, tomorrow! You don't want it to come. You don't want the date to end. Oh, Please don't end; don't end ever.[19]

Our first sexual encounter is a very potent one. It is something that everyone remembers. Barbara Walters recently asked Johnny Carson, in a televised interview, about his first sexual experience. He responded immediately, saying it happened when he was seventeen, was awful, and would Barbara like to know the girl's name? Most of us are like that. Of all the adult secrets, of all the adult activities anticipated by teenagers, sexual encounters are the ultimate challenge of maturity. Like the death of a parent, the loss of one's virginity is an experience that one can never change, and because it is something with which we are intensely emotionally involved, it is something we never forget.

Because we invest so much in this first sexual encounter, it is bound to be disillusioning; it can never live up, in either the bad or the good sense, to all that we imagined or wanted it to be. For boys, who may partly fear the experience because they worry about not performing well, the reality can be a heartening and positive disillusionment. By contrast, for girls, for whom the sexual encounter was embedded in a romantic context, a beautiful place, and a loving partner, the reality can be a startling and terribly disappointing reality. This is not true in every case, of course; there are many romantic boys and not a few young women who enjoy sex, period. But the portrayal given above holds true for the majority of teenagers. The following are the reactions of some teenagers to their first sexual experience. First, the boys:

> It was like I had become a man and I wanted to tell everyone about it.

> I felt very relaxed, drained of all worries and cares. I was proud. A little warm all over. I really enjoyed myself. I felt I'd never be the same. I had taken a step on my way to manhood.

> I felt like it was an accomplishment. I felt that I was a big boy or a man. It gave me a sense of pride. It was like growing up.

Now the girls:

> I felt guilty because I hardly knew the person I had intercourse with. The guy was older than I was and I thought he was something he was not. He sweet talked me and being a young fourteen, I fell for it.

> At first I was hurt because I felt I had lost the little girl in me.

> I was really worried about it. I wanted to do it my first time with someone I really loved so it would be more like my giving it to someone. But unfortunately, that wasn't the way it was.[20]

For boys, then, the first sexual experience is more often a positive disillusionment than a negative one. They feel that they have accomplished something they had serious doubts about, even if they did not really admit those doubts to themselves. For girls, the first sexual experience is more often a negative disillusionment because it seldom matches the romantic fantasy they had imagined. For both young men and young women, however, the experience contributes to a further clarification of self and the person's identity. If the sexual experience comes at a time when this process of forming an identity is well along, it can contribute in a positive way, becoming integrated into the young person's sense of self and others. But if it occurs early in the process of development, it cannot be easily integrated into the young person's budding sense of self. Rather, it stands as an isolated event that the teenager feels is somehow foreign and apart. Early sexual experience contributes to a patchwork sense of self.

The peer shocks associated with moving into the culture of adolescence are a necessary and inevitable experience for young people. Although these shocks can be painful at the time they occur, by and large they help the teenager clarify feelings, values, and attitudes, a necessary part of constructing a healthy sense of personal identity. When the shocks associated with initiation into the culture of adolescence are combined with those associated with thinking in a new key and the perils of puberty, the teenager is confronted by a formidable array of stresses. Clearly, teenagers need a protected time and place in society in order to learn how to deal with these issues before they move on to the responsibilities associated with adulthood. Society is no longer giving young people this period of time, however, as we shall see in the next few chapters. Rather, teenagers are unplaced, accorded a premature adulthood by default, because adult society really doesn't know what else to do with them.

Part II

Given:
A Premature
Adulthood

Chapter 5

Vanishing Markers

*T*he absence of a special place for teenagers in our society is evidenced by the progressive erosion of the "markers" of their transition status. Markers are external signs of where we stand, in Kierkegaard's lovely phrase, in "the stages on life's way."[1] Markers can be as simple as the pencil lines on the kitchen wall that mark a child's progress in height from birthday to birthday, or as complex as a well-deserved promotion after years of hard work and dedication. Markers are signs of progress to others as well as to ourselves.

We all have a "sense of becoming," of growing and changing as individuals. Markers confirm us in our sense of growing and changing. This confirmation, moreover, has to be social as well as personal. However personally gratifying the attainment of certain markers is, such attainments mean much more when accompanied by social recognition. Indeed, much of the gratification of reaching new markers is the public approval that comes with them. Confirmation, bar or bas mitzvah, graduation exercises, and the like provide a public acknowledgment that young people have attained new levels of maturity. Public recognition confirms teenagers in their sense of progress and growth. My student advisers, for example, appreciate having someone who is witness to the progress they have made from "wet behind the ears" freshmen to "worldly and sophisticated" seniors.

Markers are not only signs of progress; they are often much more. A promotion entails new responsibilities and new retraints, as well as some freedoms. The teenager who turns sixteen, for example, can apply for a driver's license and a work permit; but driving requires obedience to traffic rules, and working means keeping regular hours. In addition, since the age of sixteen connotes a fully accredited teenager and beginning adulthood, it also means an end to trick-or-treating, sledding, and many other "childish" things.

Giving up old markers also helps the young person become aware of his or her progress toward maturity. There is a direct parallel between the child of six or seven who says, "I don't believe in Santa Claus anymore," and the car-driving sixteen-year-old who says, "I don't ride bikes anymore." In both cases there is a pride in a new accomplishment and a certain disdain for an earlier belief or skill marker that is now seen as part of a period one has left behind.

If markers highlight where we have come from, they also serve as beacons for the future. To the college-bound high school student, attending college is a marker to be worked for and looked forward to. Getting married, having children, and having one's own place are still goals that many young people work toward. Markers tell us about our past, our present, our future. They tell us of our progress on life's way.

Given the importance of markers for our sense of becoming, we should be concerned at their disappearance. Teenagers, who are already under stress because of the many new demands placed on them, are further stressed when many of the markers of their "place" vanish. This is so because markers both protect teenagers against stress and lessen the kinds of stress they have to encounter. Markers protect teenagers against stress by helping them attain a clear self-definition, and they reduce stress by supplying rules, limits, taboos, and prohibitions that liberate teenagers from the need to make age-inappropriate decisions and choices.

Clothing Markers

Only a few decades ago children dressed differently from teen-agers. I recall that when I was growing up I had to wear knick-ers. At that time boys were not allowed to wear long pants until they reached the teen years. And I really wanted long pants. I remember having to wear corduroy knickers, which made a horrible noise when I walked. I looked forward eagerly to the day when I could walk back and forth to school without hearing that awful sound. At that time, too, girls were not allowed to wear long stockings, high heels, or makeup until they reached the teen years. Wearing long pants or long stock-ings was a sign that young people had reached a new stage of life.

Today, even infants wear designer diaper covers, and by the age of two or three many children are dressed like miniature versions of their parents. Similarly, girls of six and seven now often have expensive makeup kits and feel undressed if they go out of doors without their mascara and eye shadow. By the time girls are in their teen years, they are so adultlike in ap-pearance that it is hard even to guess their age. Teenage boys, too, are indistinguishable in their dress from school-age boys and young men. The ubiquity of blue jeans for all ages and all sexes has just about eliminated clothing as a marker of anything other than affluence and image consciousness.

For an already stressed teenager, the loss of clothing mark-ers is significant. There was a certain degree of pleasure in anticipating the day when I could wear long pants for the first time, when I could display to the "audience" that I had reached a new stage of maturity. It also gave a new teenager the priv-ilege of looking down upon the smaller children who had not made it yet. It was something firm, positive, secure, something a teenager could claim as a right, a useful counterpoise to all the anxiety and worry about height, nose length, acne, and so on. With the disappearance of clothing markers, teenagers lost an important index of their special place as well as the protec-tions once accorded that place.

Activity Markers

At an earlier time some activities were reserved for the teen years. Organized team sports, for instance, with uniforms, coaches, and intramural competition, were once the sole province of high school students. A young person entering high school could try out for the football, baseball, basketball, swimming, or track team. Those who qualified would later compete while the whole school (or almost the whole school) watched and cheered them on. Those who were good enough to make first or second string might even win a letter. And that letter would be sewn on a school sweater that would be worn proudly or, even more proudly, given to a friend to wear.

In preparation for those glorious days, elementary and junior high school kids played sandlot games with ragtag equipment, uneven teams, and no adults anywhere in evidence. Some kids were much better than others. Some kids were allowed to play, others not. A generous group of kids would let the uncoordinated play, a less generous group would not. Partly the play was just for the fun of it, but partly it was preparation for "making the team" in high school. Going to high school and possibly making a team was a marker to be looked forward to. Today, by contrast, even young children are involved in competitive sports and play with uniforms, coaches, scheduled series of games, and so on. Programs like Little League, Pop Warner, and Pee Wee Hockey often have more equipment, coaching, and scheduled competition than high school athletics. Another important marker of maturity—participation in organized team sports—has disappeared.

In part at least, this transformation may reflect what television has done to sports generally. With the introduction of television, sports are no longer games played for pleasure.

> The enormous revenues that have accompanied the rise of televised sports have changed almost every aspect of professional games Americans watch. Leagues in every sport have been expanded (watered down some critics would say) to take advantage of the interest TV has created. Terms such as the

free agent, option year and *holdout* have become as familiar to sports fans as *double play, T formation* or *body check*. Who could ever have imagined a summer in which there would be no major league baseball for almost two months? Yet it became a reality in 1981 thanks to the impasse created by the astronomical sums available to owners and players through TV scripts.[2]

Moreover, the high salaries and residuals (for commercials) available to players who become successful in tennis, basketball, baseball, or football can be enormously lucrative. At least some parents may be pushing their youngsters into sports at an early age in hopes of winning this jackpot.

Related to the loss of sports as a marker for young people is something equally important: a sense of spontaneity and a willingness to create games on one's own. A parent told me of an incident involving his son, who was nine and a member of a Little League team that was to play another team on Saturday morning. Both teams arrived, all the necessary equipment was there, and the playing field was reserved for them. But the coach did not show up. Rather than play on their own, the boys decided to go home. Clearly, for those youngsters, playing ball was not just getting together with friends to play a game. It was serious business. And if the coach wasn't there, there was no point in playing. The sport now belonged more to the adults involved than to the children who played.

Other activity markers have vanished as well. There are now, for example, beauty contests for four- and eight-year-old girls who are trained to walk, talk, and dress properly and to present themselves in the most attractive way possible. Again, the motivation in part may be money: parents may be hoping that young girls will some day be Miss America with all the fringe benefits that brings. Unfortunately, the number of these contests and pageants seems to be growing:

> The largest children's pageant is Miss Hemisphere, where more than one million contestants, starting at age 3 (and even including boys ages 3–8) competing in all 50 states each year

in preliminary, state and national contests. The Dream Girl Pageant, an offshoot of Miss Hemisphere, holds separate competitions in 25 states, also leading to a "national" final. A growing pageant organization is "America's Stars of Tomorrow" which holds beauty contests for babies from "0–2" and also for little boys.[3]

These "pageants" eliminate any possible value a beauty contest could have as a marker of maturity for young women. It then becomes an unmarked activity, like taking a bath, which one can do at any age.

Apparently there are no markers that are immune to being seized by younger children. The martial arts, for example, used to be reserved for teenagers and adults. But no more:

> Teenage males have been trying out for fighting ever since Bruce Lee flashed those furious fists 13 years ago. These days, however, they're being upstaged by boys and girls as young as three. At that tender age, Richard Dietrich started practicing the Tae Kwan Do at the Jhoon Rhee school in Alexandria, VA. Now a ripe old five, Richard has already earned a red belt (two notches below black), like his twelve-year-old brother, Michael.[4]

Again, in another unlikely realm—religious activities—markers have begun to disappear. In some churches, a well-intentioned clergy and parishioners allow children of any age to take communion. This means that the youngsters no longer have to be of a particular age or to have completed a specified course of instruction before they can participate in this rite. But it is clearly evident from our earlier discussion of thinking in a new key that young children cannot be expected to grasp the metaphorical significance of the wafer and the wine. Indeed one clergyman told me of a rather embarrassing incident that arose as a result of this new liberalism. A three-year-old girl chose to take communion, but when she was given the wafer she took one bite and handed it back to the priest with the explanation, "I don't like it." He ate the remainder, but wondered about the wisdom of the new policy.

As adults, we need to consider the impact of these in-fringements on teenage territory. Young people need a sense of "growing," of being in a process of transition. Birthdays are looked forward to as markers of increased maturity (not, as among adults, with dread as a sign of advancing age). Children and teenagers operate according to what I call an *age of dyna-mism;* that is, they want to be like the next older age group and not like the next younger age group. In the world of teenage romances, for example, the heroines are from fifteen to eighteen years of age, but the readers are thirteen. Not being like the younger age group and aspiring to be like the next older group is a marker of place. But when a teenager finds younger children doing what he or she never did—competing in team sports, practicing Kung Fu—the age dynamism, which is a reassuring marker of place, is lost. What should belong to the teenager has been taken by others both older and younger, and the teenager is left with nothing—no place that is special to the teenager alone.

One consequence of vanishing activity markers is already clear. There has been a rapid decline, over the last few years, in the number of teenagers who are going out for high school sports. As the marker quality of high school sports has been lost, so has its appeal to teenagers.

Innocence Markers

In a recent book entitled *The Disappearance of Childhood* Neil Postman argues that childhood is, or was, a period of innocence when children were protected and shielded from certain kinds of information.[5] In the past two decades, however, the protec-tions for children have vanished, and today's children are ex-posed to all sorts of information. Since contemporary society no longer holds the idea of childhood as a period of innocence, does that mean children have disappeared, too? And, further, if there is no place in the society for teenagers, have they dis-appeared as well?

It is important to distinguish here between the conceptions

of childhood and of adolescence held by any given society at any particular time and the reality of children and teenagers. Children and teenagers are *not* social inventions or historical discoveries. They are the young of the species, and like the young of every species, they require the care, protection, and guidance of the adults of that species if they are to survive and to flourish. The idea that children and adolescents are social inventions that can in some way be "disinvented" rests on the false assumption that society and culture are in some way separate and apart from nature. But we are biological beings, and as such we are part of biological nature. The young of our species, like the young of other species, are not social creations but rather biological facts. We can deny those facts, but the reality persists nonetheless.

It is certainly true, as Postman contends, that society no longer seems to regard children as innocent or to see childhood innocence as a positive characteristic. And it is also true that even young children are today exposed to every nuance of human vice and depravity under the mistaken assumption that this will somehow inure them to evil and prepare them to live successful, if not virtuous and honorable, lives. This assumption rests on the mistaken belief that a bad experience is the best preparation for a bad experience. In fact, just the reverse is true: *a good experience is the best preparation for a bad experience.* Innocence markers provide good experiences and their absence, too often, bad ones.

Before turning to that issue, let me make one additional point. Adults can expose children to each and every form of human depravity without destroying their innocence, for innocence comes from within, not from without. Children will interpret the information they are given in their own way and in light of their own understanding. They will preserve their innocence because they cannot truly comprehend evil. Children will resist information for which they are not prepared. Recall the Connecticut youngster who recited the Lord's Prayer as "Our father who art in New Haven, Harold be thy name." A mother told me of her hour-long effort to persuade her daughter not to go with strangers. After the long lesson the mother asked, "Do you understand?" Her daughter replied, "Yes, yes, but what is a stranger?" And a young girl talked knowingly about an older girl who had been "raked," which she thought meant "you get stuck with a fork."

Exposure to all facets of human sexuality, aggression, and degradation is not likely to destroy the innocence of young children, although it certainly must frighten them to see adults so out of control. What does result from the easy access to this type of information is a loss of its value as a marker for maturity. When such information was reserved for people who had attained a certain age or level of maturity, access to the information was an important sign of growing up. Making the information available to young children, whether they comprehend it or not, destroys its value as a marker for those who are ready for it—namely, older teenagers.

For example, today's children and teenagers have a great deal of economic information. Only a couple of decades ago a family's finances were clearly none of a child's business. If he or she asked what a parent earned, what the house cost, and so on, the youngster was given to understand that it was none of his or her affair. Today, even young children know about the family's finances, and if there is a separation or divorce, they probably know what the alimony and child-support payments are. In Detroit recently, some children tried to starve themselves when their fathers were laid off. They did not want to be a financial burden.

It makes sense to begin to share some financial information with teenagers who can understand it and appreciate it, and the information thus becomes a sign of their new maturity. But if the information is given to young people when they are children, its usefulness as a marker of maturity is lost. The same is true for family secrets. Although it makes sense to shield children from information about family members who may be alcoholic or mentally disturbed (because children cannot understand these illnesses), it does help to share this knowledge with teenagers. A teenager who is excluded from this information may experience self-doubt. Brenda, an eighteen-year-old, wrote:

> There was a secret about my cousin who had been in a mental institution for three or four years. I knew she had run away from home, but I didn't know she was in an institution. She had tried to commit suicide. I just found out about it. I've seen her since then and I think if I had known about her problem, I might have been able to help her. I wish my parents had said something. That really bothers me.[6]

As Brenda's experience illustrates, being let in on family secrets can be a useful marker of maturity for teenagers. But this value is lost if the information is given to young people when they are children (when they can't deal with it) rather than when they are teenagers (when they can deal with it).

Others signs of innocence have disappeared as well. Sexual information is now readily available even to young children. On a recent cross-country flight I was surprised to see that the movie being shown was *An Officer and a Gentleman*. My surprise came from the fact that there were many young people on the plane, ranging in age, I guessed, from three to sixteen. There were some explicit sex scenes in the film, and though the children were not sold headsets, they did not need them to figure out what was going on. The other adults, including the parents, seemed to take for granted that the children and teenagers could cope with what they were seeing. The stewardess told me that the film had been "cleaned up" for viewing on the plane, but "cleaned up" is a relative term, and the movie didn't seem that "clean" to me.

The introduction of cable television and of R-rated films available for home viewing means that children have access to nudity and heavy sexual interaction at an early age. When this happens, the role of this information as a marker is, in part at least, lost. We don't yet know the impact of this early exposure on a teenager's emerging sexuality, but we should not forget that interest in, and knowledge about, sexuality was once a marker of teenage status. When even young children talk knowingly about "making out" and "making love," the teenager must wonder how he or she differs from younger children and older teenagers. Knowledge about sexuality is a part of the teenager's developing identity that society at large has trivialized by making it so commonplace and accessible even to young children.

The innocence of children and teenagers with respect to violence has also been lost through television. As Alfred Hitchcock is reputed to have said, "Television has brought murder back into the home, where it belongs." Hitchcock, of course, was referring to the fact that murder is often between family members. But one can question whether it belongs in the homes of children where it is now so pervasive. According to one study:

> One third of all TV characters portrayed on the screen support themselves either by fighting crime or by committing it. The firing of handguns is so common that a typical night in front of the set can perhaps best be compared to an evening spent in a shooting gallery. . . . In TV's world, murders take place more frequently and crime occurs about ten times more often than in the real world.[7]

Perhaps, in order to keep up, movies have become, if not more violent than television, at least more explicit and gory.

> The trouble with most of the horror films made now is that there is no serious content. They reflect no myths, they have no center. They are just pure sensation but that is a reflection of our times because so many adults are living lives of pure sensation. Horror films aren't bad for kids, they have a good scare, especially when they go with friends and it is a group experience.[8]

The issue here is not whether watching violence and horror damages children (at the very least it "numbs them emotionally"). Rather, the issue is what this new accessibility to horror and violence to even young children does to that accessibility as a marker of teenage status. When only teenagers were permitted to see horror and violent films and programs, such viewing could be used as a sign of mature status. It was part of what a teenager could do now that he or she was grown, or partially grown, and was something that younger children could not do. Admission to the ranks of those who could watch such material without dire consequences was a rite of passage and contributed to the teenager's growing sense of himself or herself as a more responsible, more mature person. Now that even young children have ready access to horror and violence in television and movies and are assumed to be capable of handling this freedom, the value of this accessibility as a marker is lost to teenagers.

Image Markers

The images of teenagers provided by the media have changed dramatically in the last twenty years. The ways teenagers are portrayed on radio, in film, on television, in books, and in song lyrics are signs of their place in society. They tell preteens what it will be like to be a teenager, teenagers where they are, and young adults where they have been. At one time teenagers were portrayed as rather flighty, impulsive, given to rash schemes and overambitious projects, and in need of adult restraint, common sense, and good judgment. In the media today the roles have been reversed, and we now have what has come to be known as the *adultified* child. An example of the reversal of adult and teenage roles is provided by a recent television series:

> Edward Stratton 3rd is 35, wealthy, dim witted, naive and hopelessly immature. He spends his days playing video games in his private arcade and riding around his mansion atop an oversized toy train. Ricky, his 12 year old son, is a bright and sophisticated computer whiz, as responsible as dad is feckless. When Ricky tries to engage his father in serious discussion, Edward flops to his knees to demonstrate his favorite game, Swamp Wars. Asked by Ricky if the computer controlling their household gadgets has a "random access memory," Edward is the picture of slack-jawed bewilderment.[9]

Over the past decade this kind of adultified child has become increasingly common both on television and in films. In the fall of 1982, nine of the twenty-three new series premiering on prime-time television featured one or more adultified children. In the view of TV critic Sally Bedell, "Such characters transcend the winsome precocity of the Shirley Temple variety; the children in prime time tend to be miniature adults, possessing the tastes, mores, sensitivity, knowledge and even cynicism that until recent years were the exclusive province of maturity."[10]

The portrayals of adultified children are not accidental but deliberate. They grow out of a well-intentioned but confused idea about the importance of realism for young people growing up in a frightening and unpredictable world. For many TV writers and producers, realism means not only that teenagers have to be presented with every type of adult problem but also that they be portrayed as handling these problems with a kind of low-key, cool maturity. This perception is a response to what many thought were unrealistic portrayals of adults. According to Paul Junger Witt, one of the writers of ABC's family comedy series *It Takes Two*, "There is an enormous disservice to children who are impressionable to see a father who has all the answers." When people had a steady diet of *Father Knows Best* and *Leave It to Beaver*, says Mr. Witt, "I wonder how many people came away from those shows thinking that their parents had failed them."[11] In the same vein, Gary David Goldberg, creator and executive producer of *Family Ties*, writes, "I don't think we should resurrect people like Ozzie Nelson and Jim Anderson. As beautiful as they were, they're not the correct building materials for today much the way many old buildings are beautiful but not right for today's world. Society now calls for different building materials that can withstand different pressures."[12]

There is, however, an alternative to portraying children as accomplished adults or parents as all-knowing. Both children and adults should be portrayed as they are in reality. To portray children and teenagers realistically does not mean they must be depicted as complete innocents or as sophisticated jet-setters. Rather, a realistic portrayal would show children as they are, innocent in part, wise in part, crafty at times, and so on. Television is doing now what American films did for so long, namely, distorting the reality of childhood. A true perception of childhood should be presented, thereby enabling children and teenagers to explore their worlds from another perspective. As Vincent Canby writes:

> The most pertinent reality of childhood is the state of physical change, of being forever in transition in a world that may be mysterious or threatening or too big to be negotiated comfortably or that simply doesn't listen. This is something that European filmmakers have acknowledged without pretension. I think of René Clément's "Forbidden Games," Vittorio de Sica's "Bicycle Thief," David Lear's "The Red Balloon."[13]

Canby observed about Steven Spielberg's films *E.T.* and *Poltergeist:*

> The Spielberg films are distinguished from most other American films with which they might be compared by the richness of their gently satiric social detail. The gallant youngsters of "E.T." and the besieged ones of "Poltergeist" do not live in some unlocated American Never Never Land but in California in the all-too-real real estate development. The houses which look not as if they've been built but laid by a giant hen come equipped with every possible kitchen gadget, hot tubs, suspended staircases, and walls that are probably paper thin.
>
> The kids eat dreadfully over-sweetened cold cereals and waffles defrosted in toasters, and they sleep in beds that are often full of potato chips. They play with remote control toys, drink colas that rot their teeth even as they are being straightened and they go to sleep to the hum of the television sets that are no longer being watched.[14]

It would be hard to condone parents who permit such behavior, but it is at least an accurate portrayal of what goes on in many American homes.

Many movies depicting teenagers repeat the error of television and assume that realism means portraying teenagers as wise grownups and adults as dumb children. One example of this type of portrayal is the movie entitled *My Bodyguard*, which tells the story of a young adolescent boy who moves to a new city with his father and grandmother when the father takes a position as manager of a hotel. The boy is presented as intelligent, sensitive, and thoughtful. The father is depicted as rather inept, a womanizer, and bemused by life, while the grandmother is portrayed as a alcoholic and a man chaser.

The story revolves around the son, who quickly makes friends at his new school, readily wins the respect of his teachers, and is put upon by bullies. They try to extort money from him for "protection," but he refuses and is beaten up as a result. The boy then decides to hire a bodyguard to protect him from the bullies. For this role he chooses a tall, husky young man who is sullen, silent, and reputed to have killed someone. The prospective bodyguard resists the boy's overtures of friendship, but the boy perseveres.

Eventually, with the skill and verbal acumen of a trained psychotherapist, he progressively brings his friend to recount his history. The potential bodyguard describes with tears how he accidentally shot and killed his younger brother when they were playing with guns. With that catharsis, the young man becomes friendly, begins to smile, and joins his new friend in getting rid of the bullies. Together the two young men also assist the father and grandmother in their efforts to lead more integrated lives.

This type of story, whether on television or in the movies, suggests that teenagers do not need a time to learn to become adults. Rather, it suggests that teenagers are, by nature, more mature and better adapted to society than are their elders, that young people can assume a ready-made adult identity without time and effort. Not only do these portrayals deny teenagers the immaturity markers that were once synonymous with teenage life, they also encourage young people to assume adulthood because they can do certain adultlike things. In short, such portrayals encourage growth by substitution, by copying a form of behavior rather than by exploring and developing one's own feelings, values, and attitudes.

This type of movie goes even further. It turns the perception of life stages on its head and implies that it is adults, not teenagers, who need guidance, support, and wise counsel. The stress engendered by such perceptions of adults and teenagers may help to explain why the film *Kramer vs. Kramer*, which resisted this type of portrayal, has become a kind of cult film for teenagers, many of whom have seen it as often as six times. In that film the father takes charge of the situation and behaves like an adult taking care of a child. And the child is a child, not a miniature adult.

In my travels around the country I frequently meet with large groups of teenagers and talk with them about some of the things they find most worrisome. Again and again, I find that young people are victims of media images. A typical example is the twelve-year-old girl in the Midwest who told me, "My parents are always fighting. I try to help, to get them to listen to one another, to stop yelling and start talking, but I don't have too much luck. I guess it's my fault." This young woman, like many of her peers, believes that she has to adopt the role of therapist for her parents. In this case, and in many others like it, the young woman's perception of her role grew (in part, at least) from the way teenagers are depicted on television and film. She was enormously relieved when I told her that it was not her responsibility to be a therapist for her parents. She should, I suggested, tell them how frightened and unhappy their arguing makes her and how she wishes they would stop. But her responsibility as a young daughter ends there.

While earlier depictions of teenagers on television and in the movies may have been idealized, they nonetheless presented teenagers as young people with concerns appropriate to their age level, school, friendships, after-school jobs, and so on. Portraying young people realistically today does not require that they be portrayed as grownups; rather, they should be portrayed as young people in transition and not, as so often happens, as adults. When young people are depicted as adultified children, they are deprived of important time in their lives, a time that can determine the quality of their future years.

The new realism that insists upon portraying young people as full-fledged adults means they are confronted with "every conceivable adult problem from sex, alcohol and drugs to concerns about the environment and nuclear war."[15] Certainly we cannot and should not prevent young people from learning about the dangers of this world. But when young people are portrayed as fully competent to deal with these complex adult issues, they are dissuaded from seeking the adult support, guidance, and reassurance they so badly need to deal with such matters. They are deprived of those images of adolescent awkwardness and insecurity that make their own awkwardness and insecurity more bearable. Without signs of the boundaries of their protected world, and with images that suggest that their powers are limitless, teenagers may never seek the guidance they need and may expose themselves to stresses for which they are totally unprepared.

Authority Markers

Another important marker of a teenager's place in the social order is his or her place vis-à-vis adult authority. True authority is based upon superior competence, wisdom, and experience. Power, in contrast, is based upon superior force. A number of recent changes in our society have undermined the authority of both parents and teachers, the two classes of adults with whom teenagers interact the most. When these adults lose their authority, their claim to superior competence, wisdom, and authority, teenagers lose an all-important marker of their place in the social order.

In many ways, the next two chapters deal with the contemporary decline in the authority of both parents and teachers. Those chapters, however, are concerned with the specific unplacing effects of declining adult authority in the contemporary family and school. Here we need to recognize its marker quality and that it can be looked at as another way in which the society as a whole is becoming homogenized with respect to age and authority. Such homogenization deprives teenagers of still another important marker of their once-special status.

Consider for a moment what divorce does to the teenager's sense of parental wisdom, competence, and experience. This event not only confronts teenagers with difficult problems of self-definition, but it also changes their perception of adult authority. Many teenagers think, for example, that because their parents have messed up their own lives, they have nothing to teach the teenager about life and love. And when, in some single-parent homes, teenagers are treated as total equals to the remaining parent, this also contributes to the decline of parental authority. (Such equal treatment is particularly perilous in early adolescence, when young people badly need the guidance and direction of a more knowledgeable adult.)

A more pervasive contributor to the decline of parental authority is the media. Although the impact of television on children has been widely debated, its perhaps most serious impact has often been overlooked. More than anything else, television has contributed to the decline of parental authority. Television is much too pervasive for parents to monitor and control. Unlike television in most foreign countries, where it is on for a limited number of hours each day, we have television twenty-four hours a day. And in this country there is at least one television set, and often more, for every family in the country. Without being with children almost every minute it is almost impossible for parents to monitor television viewing effectively.

This parental impotence with respect to television has quickly spread to films, books, audio tapes, and most recently the "rock videos" that promote particular songs and rock groups. Advertisers were quick to sense this new feeling of parental impotence with respect to the media. As a consequence we have an ever-increasing flood of advertisements directed at teenagers (who have the largest disposable income of any age group in this country) that have sexual innuendo as an overriding motif. The more such advertising appears, the more powerless parents feel to control it, and the process feeds upon itself.

Parents now accede to their teenagers' wishes to see films like *Ridgemont High, Porky's, Risky Business,* and, more recently, *Angel* (high school honor student by day, prostitute at night). Likewise, rock videos have become a new force to contend with. They are usually short, just a few minutes, and often quite violent or sexual, or both. They are now being strung together into hour-long programs that seem to have teenagers mesmerized. There is no plot or story, no consistent characters, just a lot of action. Many young people tell me that peers who watch these videos for an hour or so become "hyper" and "cranky."

So popular have the sex and violence materials for teenagers become, and so widespread parental impotence, that even the venerable Disney Studios—once the epitome of family-oriented films—is turning to a kind of soft porn for teenagers (under a different label, of course):

> For the last two years, profits from Walt Disney Productions new films have been strictly Mickey Mouse. . . . Figuring that prime moviegoers—those of high school and college age—have been put off by the wholesomeness of the Disney image, the company announced a name change last week and promised some films with some unDisney-like spice. . . .

The first of the studio's more mature and provocative films is something called *Splash*. The studio described it as a "sensuous love story." And a studio executive, Mr. Berger, made the studio's purpose quite clear. "The teenage market is the major audience out there," he said, "and we have to find a way to get to them."[16] In effect, the media has taken a great deal of control over what teenagers see and hear away from parents and have thus undermined their authority.

It is not only parents whose authority has declined in recent times. The authority of teachers has diminished as well.

> Relations between the lay public and the teaching profession . . . changed in significant ways. In the 1940's, few teachers belonged to a union; strikes were uncommon; adminis-

trators were powerful within their school building or their
district and in hiring, promoting and assigning teachers.
Though their pay was low, teachers had more education than
did the parents of their students and commanded the respect
that went with the authority they wielded. Teaching attracted
a number of gifted women, for whom career opportunities
were limited. In some communities, there were substantial
restrictions placed on teachers' behavior; as models for the
community's youth, teachers were expected not to smoke or
drink or otherwise set a bad example.[17]

It is hardly necessary to compare that description with what
obtains for teachers today. There has been a radical change in
the respect and authority that were once accorded teachers by
both students and parents.

The new technologies, particularly computers, have added
to the decline of teacher authority. What has disrupted teachers
most is the speed with which personal computers have become
part of children's home environment. As a consequence, many
students are far more proficient in computers than their teachers are. And schools are not sure which way to go with computers, only that they should have some around. The intimi-
dation of teachers and schools by computers is not lost on
young people. They see it as still another sign of adult inability
to manifest wisdom, competence, and experience in a productive way.

The importance of adult authority for the teenager's growth
by differentiation and integration can hardly be overestimated.
When teenagers interact with adults whose authority they respect, they can have productive, if painful, battles over ideas
and actions. Such adults provide healthy opponents against
whom to test their own opinions and values. But when adult
authority is undermined or lost, the adult is no longer marked
as one to be attended to and to learn from. The generations
have become homogenized and the special status of being a
teenager has been lost, and with it an important opportunity
for growth by differentiation and integration.

112

Vanishing markers, then, give ample evidence that there is no special place for teenagers in today's society. Markers such as clothing, activities, innocence, media image, and adult authority have all but disappeared as signs of the teenager's special place in society. The disappearance of these markers deprives young people of important learning experiences for the elaboration of an integrated sense of self and identity. As we shall see later, the absence of markers also confronts teenagers with powerful stressors because of the new freedoms that are provided. We need to look now at another phenomenon of today's society that also impairs identity formation while adding stress to teenagers' lives: family permutations.

Chapter 6

Family Permutations

Webster's Dictionary defines the word *permutation* as a "major or fundamental change based primarily on rearrangement of existing elements." In the past several decades many American families have undergone some major rearrangements of their existing elements, namely, parents and children. When such rearrangements occur, children and teenagers tend to lose their special place in the family structure. In the traditional family of two parents and assorted children, the adults were the authority as well as the repositories of wisdom, good judgment, patience, and tolerance. When the family is permuted, usually as a consequence of divorce, the traditional order of things is changed. In the permuted family, the adults often lose their authority as well as their claim to the attributes of maturity. In some permuted families, the children and teenagers are more like adults than are their parents.

Before we look at how such family permutations affect teenagers in their struggle to define themselves as individuals, we need to get some idea about the extent of the problem, about how many families in the United States are undergoing permutations. John Naisbitt's *Megatrends* gives us a rough idea of how many teenagers are being affected in this way.

> Most of us were raised in a typical nuclear family: Father was breadwinner, mother took care of the house and children,

usually two. But today there is no such thing as a typical family. And only a distinct minority (7 percent) of America's population fits the traditional family profile.

Today's family can be a single parent (male or female) with one or more children, a two-career couple with no children, a female breadwinner with child and househusband, or a blended family that consists of a previously married couple and a combination of children from these two previous marriages.[1]

These various marital rearrangements have removed teenagers from their once-privileged position within the family and have led to two different but related consequences. First, because divorce is a shock to the teenager's system, he or she often becomes so preoccupied with the issue that he or she focuses solely on the divorce and neglects the age-appropriate concerns related to the construction of a healthy identity. Second, and perhaps more important, divorce changes the teenager's status not only within the family but also outside it, with friends, teachers, and relatives. A young person's position in these relationships is an important part of his or her self-definition. In effect, therefore, the teenager's new social status as a result of divorce complicates the task of identity formation— it forces him or her to rework elements of the definition of his or her identity that were already well in place. The teenager in effect must start over when the struggle is the hardest.

Separation and Divorce

At one time, separation and divorce were uncommon experiences and spoken of in hushed tones, if they were discussed at all. Today, separation and divorce are treated by many as commonplace experiences, and, indeed, statistics now support this attitude. The number of children and teenagers affected by divorce and separation more than doubled between 1970 and 1979. Moreover, it has been estimated that one million young people each year experience divorce and separation. According to the U.S. Census Bureau, 12.6 million children under the age of eighteen live with only one parent; that figure represents 20.1 percent of all children.

The effect of separation and divorce upon teenagers differs from their effect upon children. Teenagers, thanks to their ability to think in a new key, can appreciate the full impact of divorce—its emotional, personal, social, and financial repercussions. By contrast, children are protected from these multiple concerns by their limited mental abilities. They know something is wrong, they appreciate and suffer from the absence of a parent, but they cannot and do not anticipate what the future will bring as a consequence.

It is not simply because teenagers can imagine all the ramifications of divorce that divorce is perhaps harder on them than upon their younger siblings. In addition, their new capacity to find fault with their parents is reinforced mightily if parents separate. Young people seem to say to themselves, "You see, I knew it, I knew he [or she] was like that." The separation and divorce may dangerously confirm the teenager's negative evaluations of the parent that under other circumstances might be tempered over time. Not surprisingly, the results of one study of 421 undergraduate students concluded that "parents from families broken by divorce were consistently more negatively evaluated than were parents from either intact families or families where the father had died. These findings held regardless of whether or not the mother had remarried and regardless of the sex of the students doing the evaluations."[2]

To understand the profound impact divorce can have upon teenagers, consider the reactions of some young people to first learning about their parents' divorce. For these three teenagers, the prospect of divorce means changes difficult to imagine and painful to consider.

> *Janie, 14:* When my parents told me about their divorce plans, I couldn't believe it! I kept thinking that they really didn't have to do it. Sure they didn't get along, but couldn't we all learn to live with it? I couldn't really face the idea of how things, my life, I mean, would change.

Vicky, 17: At first, when I thought about my parents' divorce I was kind of relieved. At least the terrible fighting would be over. But then I tried to imagine how it would be for my mother and me to live on our own. Could we make it? I wanted to go to college. Where would the money come from?

Gene, 15: My reaction to my parents' divorce was to go to my room. Partly I was hiding out and partly sulking. I didn't come out for more than a day. I just kept comparing my family to my friends who were staying together. Why couldn't we be happy like that? I really blamed my parents for the trouble they were going to cause me.[3]

Although the effects of separation and divorce on teenagers are traumatic at least for a while, a majority find the new arrangement an acceptable alternative to their parents' remaining together under certain circumstances. In one study, three out of four teenagers said divorce was justified if parents argue all the time, physical violence is involved, or one or both parents are unfaithful.[4] Teenagers recognize, therefore, that some kinds of parental interactions can be even more distressing than divorce and separation.

The impact of separation and divorce upon teenagers is compounded by the understandable but regrettable tendency of parents to deny the problem or avoid discussing the topic at length and in detail with their offspring. This type of open discussion can be an important part of the teenager's effort to deal with an emotional situation. Such discussions give the teenager a chance to express his or her feelings and to begin to make the emotional and intellectual adjustments required by the new social position. The teenager has to begin to think of himself or herself in new terms—"Now I am a child of divorce"—and to face the trepidation of communicating this to friends and teachers.

Such revelations and reevaluations are exceedingly painful because they are witnessed by a judgmental imaginary audience. They also involve tortured changes in the personal fable, briefly expressed by the statement "Other kids' parents will divorce, not mine!" In addition, the teenager must struggle with a new personal evaluation and a new evaluation of his or her parents. Separation and divorce are difficult enough by themselves; their negative effects should not be multiplied by a secrecy that makes it even more difficult for teenagers to come to grips with their new status and to incorporate it within an evolving sense of identity. The teenager cannot be misled, deceived, or kept in ignorance for very long, and these actions can have their own consequences for the parents. Consider this description of how a sixteen-year-old girl learned about her parents' impending divorce:

> I don't disapprove of the divorce but I believe that parents shouldn't just spring it on their kids. I had to find out from my grandmother when my parents got divorced. We came up from Florida when I was eleven. Mom was just settling into the house and we spent a lot of time with my grandmother. She told us. I thought my parents were just spending some time away from each other, but my mom moved away and took us.[5]

This girl was not informed of the decision to divorce and move to another area. At a time when she was capable of understanding, she was simply ignored.

There are as many different divorce stories as there are families undergoing the change. Each family and each story is unique. Nonetheless, even in the most accommodating of divorces, the probability that divorce will be an unsettling experience for the teenagers is great. For whether the divorce is amicable (rare) or bitter (usual), there is at least one common consequence: teenagers lose the privileged status of belonging to an intact family. The two-parent family is still the model for teenagers, and they see and value this type of family as the norm. If their parents separate, they feel that they are different (in a bad way) from their peers.

The frequency of divorce in America has not made this experience any easier for teenagers to bear. It doesn't really help if a friend's parents are divorced too, just as a friend's having a toothache does not reduce the pain of one's own. Moreover, the commonness of divorce has not removed any of the barriers to identity formation that divorce inevitably brings with it. The high incidence of separation and divorce means only that many more teenagers are struggling with new and heavier burdens of stress.

Single-Parent Households

The experience of divorce and separation has to be distinguished from the experience of living in an altered or permuted household. It is not unlike the difference between a wedding and what comes after. The wedding is a public event, which is announced and changes one's status in relation to other people. The wedding creates a marriage, but that is a separate and different fact from what passes in the home between the newly married partners. Moreover, adopting the proper attitude, as a newly married person, to present to the outside world is different from adjusting to the fact of marriage, of living with another person day after day. The same is true for divorce. It is one thing for the teenager to adapt his or her attitude outside the home to the changed status and quite another to adapt to his or her changed position within the home. The divorce may be announced, the teenager may outwardly appear to accept it, but in the home day after day the teenager must struggle to live in a new situation.

Once the family is reconstituted, new living arrangements are made if necessary, new life-styles are established (this usually occurs within one to two years after divorce), and new barriers to successfully defining an identity can, but need not, emerge. The most serious barrier may be the needs of the parent. As I pointed out in my book *The Hurried Child*, the single parent is in a difficult position and may be tempted to use a young child as someone to share with and confide in. With teenagers, in contrast, the single parent may often demand that the son or daughter serve as a kind of social conscience. When single parents engage in behavior that even they know, at some level, is outlandish, they may nonetheless expect their children to accept it and to give it their approval.

Although one can understand the pain many single parents experience and their need to vent their anger and frustration in some public way, they should not conduct their lives at the teenager's expense. Too often this is precisely what happens. In my clinical work I see single parents who engage in behavior that contrasts glaringly to their behavior prior to their divorce. They seem impervious to what this behavior does to their teenage children and demand that their offspring accept and condone their actions without question. This is clearly unreasonable and places the teenager in an untenable position—approving of behavior by a person who once taught the teenager that such behavior was wrong. The following case study from my files will illustrate the problem (I have disguised the information to protect the people involved):

> Mrs. K. is an attractive woman in her middle to late thirties. She has recently divorced her physician husband and retained custody of her teenage daughter. As part of the divorce settlement, she also kept the family home, a large house in a rather exclusive suburb. The daughter came in for consultation in connection with her frequent running away from home, often with older men. She relates that her mother has a boyfriend who is younger than the mother and whom the daughter describes as a "ski bum" who swaggers about the house with a beer can and torn undershirt, because he "thinks he looks like Marlon Brando in *A Streetcar Named Desire.* The daughter also says that he makes passes at her whenever the mother isn't around. To make matters worse, the mother and her boyfriend have wild parties that disturb the neighbors and embarrass the daughter. She feels she can no longer bring her friends home.

In this case the mother wanted her daughter to understand and to support her actions, to serve as an approving conscience, as it were. This put the daughter in an impossible situation. If she used the new information about her mother to further differentiate her conception of her mother from that of herself, the results would be destructive, tearing apart much of the positive work she had already accomplished in defining her own identity. On the other hand, if she simply went along with her mother and substituted new values for old ones, this would be destructive too. As in many cases of this type, the mother was too much involved with her own pain to be able to provide her daughter the support and guidance she required. Instead, the mother could only reverse the roles and demand that the daughter support her new relationship. Before we were able to remove the daughter from the situation, she ran away again. When she returned she was already three months pregnant. She had just turned fifteen.

The degree of problem behavior exhibited by teenagers in homes of divorce is in part a measure of the pain and conflict engendered by a parent's unexpected behavior following divorce. I have seen many examples of this. In one instance a divorced mother became pregnant and for religious reasons decided to have the baby. She had broken up with the baby's father, one of a series of lovers taken after the divorce. She now expected her teenage son and daughter to accept their new stepbrother and her behavior without question. Indeed, she expected them to support her in her decision and to condone her actions. Not surprisingly, both teenagers eventually ended up as wards of the court, the girl for sexual delinquency and vagrancy, the boy for alcoholism.

Fathers, of course, are also responsible for exposing teenagers to this kind of problem. Many teenagers are caught in impossible situations when their fathers marry women much younger than themselves, women who are much closer to the teenagers in age and orientation. At the very least, this can be embarrassing to the son or daughter. When there is a physical attraction between the teenage son and his father's new wife, or when the teenage daughter bitterly resents a rival for the attention of her boyfriends, the situation can become explosive. In one instance a teenage girl attacked her stepmother and had to be placed in a detention center. That experience alone undid much of the positive self-definition she had constructed before her father's remarriage.

122

These may be extreme cases, but they illustrate how new family configurations can affect the teenager's effort to form an identity. For most teenagers, the teen years represent a time of exploring safely the intricacies of personal relationships with friends and peers. They really cannot cope with involvement in relationships with less innocent adults, adults who are often emotionally usurping the time that belongs to the teenager.

There are, by contrast, some teenagers who find that living in a single-parent home can be better than living in a two-parent home. The conflicted two-parent home can bring unbearable pain and confusion to the children and teenagers involved. Joanne, aged fifteen, explained:

> Now that my Mom and I are alone together, it's really peaceful. I don't have two parents telling me what to do all the time. I don't have to wait for my mother to consult with my father or vice versa. They never agreed anyway! Now when I ask my mother a question, she answers. It's a lot easier now.

A seventeen-year-old girl writes:

> The only difference I can see living with my mom alone is that my sister, who's nine, tends to be more affectionate toward guys. I think she misses my father more than I do. But, then, she never knew what he did to my mother. She only remembers the good times because she was always asleep when they argued and hit.

For these two girls and others, divorce brought the end of a problem and meant a new quality in their home life.

For other teenagers, the single-parent home can bring new responsibilities—when appropriate and not overpowering—that can contribute to the growth of a sense of competence and self-confidence. Allen, aged sixteen, grew from the experience:

> I've got a lot more freedom now and my mother says that I am the man of the house. There's nobody that can tell me what to do, either physically or verbally, and you feel a lot

123

more sense of yourself. My brother feels the same way. I don't think he really liked having my dad around either.[6]

The new arrangements in the home thus can prompt the teenager to grow into them, to reach another level of maturity that might not have been attainable at home before the divorce.

Separation and divorce and living with a single parent are often harder for the young teenager than for the older one. The young teenager is so concerned with the imaginary audience that any deviation from the assumed "norm" of family life leads to extreme embarrassment and self-consciousness about the family. As teenagers become older and more experienced, the "audience" loses some of its power. John, sixteen years old, expressed this quite well:

> I miss my father, but I know my parents were unhappy together so I guess it was the best thing that they split. It's no big deal living with just my mom. I didn't like it as much when I was younger because the other kids would talk about their fathers and I couldn't. But now a lot of the kids I know have parents who are divorced.[7]

Human beings are adaptable creatures, and most youngsters eventually are reconciled to the new living arrangements entailed by divorce and separation. Nevertheless, adapting to a new life-style and a new social status complicates the task of identity formation and can deprive youngsters of valuable time needed for the task. Yet, as some of the preceding comments by young people suggest, the reverse can also sometimes be true. In families torn by daily conflict, divorce may give the teenager more rather than less time to work on self-definition. Divorce might also help clarify the teenager's conception of himself or herself and of the parents. In other words, although the new life-styles occasioned by divorce present added barriers to identity formation, these barriers are sometimes less formidable than those imposed by a two-parent family in continuous conflict.

This is important to remember. It is an unfortunate fact

that many studies seem to pinpoint divorce and separation as the main culprit when problem behavior is exhibited by young people. But this is hardly the case. The increase in problem behavior in young people today—and we will look at this in more detail later—cannot be attributed to any single cause. Rather it has to be seen as a product of *all* the many different social forces that operate to deprive teenagers of much-needed time for clarifying who they are and what their feelings, values, beliefs, and goals are. It is not separation and divorce by themselves that account for the frightening amount of problem behavior among contemporary teenagers. Only when we consider the effects of family permutations in the context of other institutions that also deprive teenagers of their special place do we get a fuller, more complete picture of what is happening to young people today.

Blended Families

The unplacing effects of divorce and separation, and of living with a single parent, can be followed by an even more unplacing experience—becoming a member of a stepfamily. Stepfamilies are among the fastest-growing permutations of the American family today.

> Divorces in the U.S. are being granted at a rate of about 1.2 million a year and most involve minor children. Some 75 percent of divorced persons remarry within five years. Adding remarriages stemming from the deaths of spouses, it's calculated that about eight million children in this country now live in stepfamilies, or about 13 percent of all children.
> By one estimate, if present rates of childbearing, divorce and remarriage continue as many as half of today's children could be involved in a stepfamily as a child or parent sometime in their lives.[8]

Stepfamilies produce identity problems for all of the parties involved, but teenagers are the most vulnerable. To put their problem in perspective, we have to acknowledge that stepparenting is far from easy for either the stepfather or the stepmother. For example, the stepmother most fight against the stereotype of the "wicked stepmother" that children have acquired from such fairy tales as "Snow White," "Cinderella," and "Hansel and Gretel." Fictional stepmothers are always cruel to their stepchildren and favor their own children. Research seems to support the view that real stepmothers have serious difficulties with stepchildren, particularly with teenage children. In a study of two thousand Florida teenagers, one-fourth of the teenagers in intact natural families reported "significant stress" at home. In homes with a stepfather or a single parent, this proportion rose to one-third. But in homes with a stepmother, the number of teenagers who reported "significant stress" rose to one-half.[9]

These statistics may reflect the fact that many custodial stepmothers are not happy with their roles. Several different factors probably account for this situation. For one thing, the custodial stepmother spends more time in child rearing than the custodial stepfather. She thus spends more time raising another woman's child or children, and is therefore more likely to be a target of the child's resentment of the divorce and altered family. Moreover, stepmothers are often considerably younger than their husbands. The husband's children are thus likely to be older, and the age gap may be too small to enable the mother to exert effective discipline. For example, I counseled a family in which the father was forty-eight and the wife was thirty-one. She had serious trouble with his three children, aged fifteen, nineteen, and twenty-one.

Although stepfathers are not burdened by negative stereotypes, they face other problems. Since the mother retains custody in 90 percent of the divorces and, frequently, the family residence as well, the stepfather usually moves into his second wife's home, which is already an existing household. The stepfather may thus be seen as an intruder or an interloper, a stranger who doesn't really belong. In addition, if he has children of his own who have remained with his former wife, he may feel guilty about giving more fatherly attention to his stepchildren than to his own. More commonly, however, most stepfathers succeed reasonably well in their new role. A stepfather may be more thoughtful and detached in his parenting than the biological father, and this can have advantages for both stepfather and stepchild. Consider the words of one stepfather:

> I recently became a stepfather to an 11 year old girl. I am fond of her and look forward to developing a meaningful and close relationship. I realize this can take time and don't expect us to adjust to each other overnight. I knew her last year when her mood was generally easy going. Now she is quite emotional and quick to argue. My wife says that this is not only the adjustment but that this is also part of preadolescence.[10]

This stepfather could deal with the preadolescent changes in his stepdaughter with perhaps greater distance than might be possible for the biological father. The stepfather comes to the relationship without any habits or established views on how to treat his child, and this allows both to come to see the other as separate and complete human beings.

Even though stepfathers may have decided advantages, Paul Bohanna, a researcher at the University of Southern California, found that stepfathers rated their performance as stepfathers lower than did either their wives or stepchildren. He interprets this result to mean that if the stepfathers do well, "it's taken for granted—that they don't hear much about it."[11] This is unfortunate, since a man's ability to succeed as a stepparent can be important in helping the teenager succeed in his or her own struggles for growth.

Young people have their own complaints about stepparents, and it is important for the health of the family that these feelings be heeded. A typical complaint is this by a teenage girl:

> John, my stepfather, goes around introducing me to his friends as "my daughter." I've asked him to stop, but he doesn't listen. I have a real father who loves me, so what is John trying to prove? I think John's a terrible insensitive person and an intruder. I'll never forgive him.[12]

127

This girl does not want to feel she is losing her relationship with her natural father; she has made his role in her life a clear part of her identity, and this should be recognized.

Here is another complaint, this time against a stepmother:

> My stepmother, Francine, is a real cold fish. The only time she kisses or hugs me is when she's trying to get me to bad mouth my sister Jill (and vice versa). Jill and I used to go along with it, until we figured out that it was dumb to sacrifice our good, close relationship for Francine's fake affection.
>
> Francine also talks about the house where we lived when my mom was alive in a really mean way. She refers to it as "stupid" and "tacky" and says mom's old furniture is "not worth saving."
>
> Jill and I wanted Dad to remarry, because we were hoping for a new mom. But why did he have to fall for her—she's nothing but an old icicle heart.[13]

This situation seems especially unfortunate, since both daughters were prepared to accept a new mother.

Becoming a member of a stepfamily is stressful for everyone involved. And each person, parent and child, has his or her own special problems with this new living arrangement. The real difficulty is, of course, that no one comes to the situation fresh, as it were. Each person comes from a well-defined place in another living arrangement, and because the place in the stepfamily is new and uncomfortable, the old place looks even better than it perhaps really was. Nonetheless, despite the many problems, a new family is constructed.

In the process of building a new family, it is usually the teenagers who suffer most. Children are not seeking identity so much as security, and the new stepparent tries hard to provide that. And even though the stepparents have to accommodate some changes in their role and in their self-definition, they usually do so on the basis of a well-established sense of personal identity. But for the teenager, the blended family presents special problems. As Florida State researcher Kay Kolvan says, "Adolescents are going through so many changes of their own that they have a special need for stability at home, and a parent's remarriage always upsets that at first."[14] Becoming a member of a blended family may shake up some of the teen-ager's established elements of his or her identity. Suppose a boy is the oldest in his family and is accustomed to being looked up to by his younger siblings. His parents divorce and his mother remarries. If there are children older than he is in the blended family, he may lose his position as the eldest. The younger siblings may look to the older stepbrother or stepsister for guidance. Such an eventuality forces the teenager to re-evaluate himself and the loyalty of his siblings. The respect of his siblings had been a source of pride, and loss of their respect may become a source of shame or unhappiness.

Again, the overt affection between the natural parent and the stepparent can raise unexpected problems. If teenagers re-tain their attachment to the biological father or mother, wit-nessing displays of affection between one parent and what amounts to a stranger can be upsetting. It raises questions about emotional ties, about loyalty, and about one's own values. Thus, for teenagers, being a part of a blended family complicates the task of building an identity by raising issues that might never have been raised had their family remained intact. In addition, the time and energy taken up in adapting to the new blended family must of necessity reduce the time and energy available to invest in the process of constructing a personal identity.

Although adjusting to a stepfamily is difficult for everyone, with goodwill and effort the problems can be resolved with positive benefits for all involved. But it does take time, usually two to four years, says psychologist Judith Wallerstein, who is executive director of the Center for the Family in Transition.

> I've had people tell me about "miraculous transformations" in their relations between them and their stepchildren—how indifference or hostility suddenly turns to liking and even love. I have to tell them it isn't really miraculous, that it happens all of the time. If the parents in a stepfamily recognize from the outset that everything isn't going to go smoothly and show patience with one another and the kids when upsets occur, they usually manage to work things out.[15]

The experience of being a member of a stepfamily, like the experience of living in a single-parent household, thus places special demands upon the teenagers. Nonetheless, most teenagers can handle these demands and get on with the task of defining themselves as people. If in other aspects of their lives the demands are not excessive, the teenager will cope successfully with the challenges he or she faces. It is only when teenagers are unplaced by other institutions within the society that experiences such as divorce, single-parent homes, and blended families can contribute to teenage problem behavior.

Teenage Mothers

Another family permutation that has always been with us but is much more prevalent today is the unwed teenage mother. As we noted earlier, the number of sexually active teenage girls has more than tripled in the last twenty years. One consequence of this increased sexual activity is a comparable increase in teenage pregnancy and child rearing. This is true despite the availability of contraception and abortion. Apparently the increased sexual activity of teenagers has not been accompanied by a comparable increase in the effective use of contraceptives.

The following statistics indicate the magnitude of the problem. One researcher, Tietze, estimated that among girls who were fourteen in 1978, 40 percent would experience a teenage pregnancy, 20 percent would give birth, and 15 percent would have an abortion by age nineteen. Of the approximately 1,142,000 teenage pregnancies in 1978, 38 percent terminated in abortions, 13 percent in miscarriages, 22 percent in out-of-wedlock births, 10 percent in legitimate but premaritally conceived births, and 17 percent in legitimate births conceived within marriage.[16]

Although the number of teenage pregnancies has increased in the last decade, the number of teenagers who carry to term has not risen. This is largely attributable to the availability of abortion. In the five years following the Supreme Court decision of 1973 and the subsequent legalization of abortion, there was a 60 percent increase in abortions by women fifteen to nineteen years old and a 120 percent rise for those under fifteen. Nonetheless, the rate of out-of-wedlock childbearing is rising for both younger and older teenagers. (Apparently abortion and contraception are used more consistently by married teenagers than by unwed teenagers.)[17]

Many explanations have been offered for teenage pregnancy. These explanations include (1) the desire to have someone to love and to be loved by in return (the infant as a toy or pet), (2) the need to be regarded as an adult (the infant as a maturity symbol), (3) the resolution of the Oedipal conflict (the infant as witness to the liberation from parental attachments), and (4) the desire to be independent (the infant as a flag of victory and freedom in the battle with parents). Although there may well be some truth to all of these explanations, they are not the whole story. As we saw in Chapter 2, young teenagers have a heavy investment in the personal fable, the belief that they are special and shielded by a cloak of invulnerability. Many young teenagers who get pregnant never believed it would happen to them. Once pregnant, however, many teenage girls rationalize or make up good reasons to justify their pregnancies. But these after-the-fact explanations are not the real reasons.

Any complete explanation of the high rate of teenage pregnancy would have to take into account many different contributing factors, such as the increased proportion of teenage girls who are sexually active, the economy, the family background, the group of young people the teenager associates with, and so on. These same conditions may help to explain why the rate of teenage marriage to legitimize pregnancy is declining. In part this is a result of the earlier age at which pregnancy is occurring, since boys and girls younger than fifteen are prevented by law from either marrying or working full time.

If there is professional disagreement about the causes of teenage pregnancy, there is complete consensus about its outcome. And this consensus is that premature parenthood has negative effects for mother, child, and family. To illustrate some of these negative effects, here are a few more statistics:

> The death rate for infants born to teenagers is 2.4 times that for infants born to older mothers and the maternal death rate is 1.6 times as great to teenagers as for others. A comparison of teenage pregnancies in New York State from 1974 to 1978 with pregnancies of women in their twenties reveals twice as great a risk of death to babies in their first year of life, and the teenager's infant death rate is greater even than that of mothers in their 40's, who are known to face increased risks. Moreover, the maternal death rate of those under 15 is two and one-half times that of those aged 20–24 (18.0 versus 7.1 deaths per 100,000 live births).[18]

For teenage mothers and infants who survive birth, there are more risks, and these risks are also high. Teenage mothers aged sixteen or younger are more likely than mothers in their early twenties to have babies with low birth weights, that is, 5.5 pounds or less. Low birth weight is, in turn, associated with many lifelong disabilities, such as cerebral palsy, mental retardation, deafness, blindness, and motor impairment. These risks to the infant are increased when the mother fails to receive proper prenatal care, and this is more likely if the girl is poor, nonwhite, and unmarried.

The impact on the teenage mother's progress toward a healthy sense of personal identity is equally dismal. Her educational prospects, important for the occupational component of her definition of self, are a case in point. Teenage mothers are twice as likely to drop out of school as nonteenage mothers. Once out of school, few teenage mothers ever return. This is true regardless of the economic circumstance of the girl's family or her ethnic background. It has been found that from one-half to two-thirds of the girls who drop out of high school give pregnancy or marriage as the main reason for terminating their education.[19]

The economic and personal consequences of the lower educational attainment of teenage mothers are predictable. With few job skills and an infant to care for, many teenage mothers are not able to find a job that pays more than the amount they can receive from welfare. But accepting welfare damages a young woman's sense of herself and her independence. Even those teenagers who marry are not much better off. They usually do not complete their education, and the risk of divorce in such marriages is considerably higher than it is in marriages of young women who marry in their twenties. The teenage mother is trapped in a web of circumstances that make it almost impossible for her to attain the integrated sense of self and the standard of living that she might have reached had she not become pregnant.

Finally, let us consider the consequences for the infant. Even if the child survives all the physical risks, the future is equally bleak. Studies of students born to teenage mothers bear this out. In comparison to students whose mothers were in their twenties when they were born, students whose mothers were teenagers scored lower on tests of mental ability, got lower grades, and had lower educational hopes and aspirations. Moreover, again in comparison to young people who were born when their mothers were in their twenties, the offspring of teenage mothers attain lower levels of education, marry at an earlier age, and divorce more frequently.[20] The evidence is clear: teenage pregnancy seriously impairs both the mother's and the child's prospects for a healthy development of a productive and fulfilling life.

The impact of a pregnancy on the teenage mother's evaluation of herself can be better understood if we look at some of the reactions of relatives. Since our self-evaluations are, in part at least, composed of the evaluations others have of us, bad evaluations can make a positive definition of oneself hard to achieve. Consider the following letter to Ann Landers's advice column from a new grandfather.

> Dear Ann Landers: Please do not congratulate me on becoming a grandfather. My daughter who had the baby is not married and you know it. The girl gave up her chance

for an education, a good future and the respect of her friends and relatives for a no-good bum.

The father of my grandchild dropped out of school in the 10th grade. He has no job and no ambition, nor is he interested in getting trained so he can support himself, or the girl he made pregnant.

The only reason I have permitted our daughter and her bastard brat to live under our roof is because my soft hearted wife begged and pleaded with me not to throw them out on the street. I have no use for this weak, stupid girl who has denied me the joy of walking her down the aisle and giving her in marriage to a decent man I could be proud of.

To put it bluntly. Congratulations are not in order. Our daughter is a tramp.[21]

Such attitudes, unfortunately, are more often the rule than the exception. Although it would be wrong to excuse the teenage mother from any and all responsibility, some compassion is in order. The teenage mother's struggle toward an understanding of herself has already been halted by the problem of having to incorporate a concept of motherhood into a sense of self that is still only partly formed. Successful mothering requires a woman who has a secure sense of identity, one that will allow her to give herself to another person without fear of losing herself. The young woman described in the letter will have an even harder time achieving any kind of integrated concept of self if even those aspects of identity she could once take for granted (beloved daughter) are now brought into question. Further, whatever problem led to her early pregnancy will remain unsolved while the young mother struggles merely to keep up with the reality of her situation—caring for her child and herself and coping with her father's virulent disapproval.

We know much less about teenage fathers than we do about teenage mothers. In the few studies that have been done, it has been found that teenage fathers experience stress as a consequence of being a prospective parent. They worry about financial responsibilities, parenting skills, education, employment, transportation, relationship with girlfriends, and facing life in general.[22] In some cases these concerns are expressed by efforts to marry the girl, or at least to maintain the relationship and provide some emotional and financial support.

The family permutation of the unmarried teenage mother is an unhappy one for all concerned. For the young mother and father it is an unplacing experience that seriously impairs their efforts to develop a healthy sense of personal identity. To be in the place of a parent while still being, in many respects, a child, to be in the place of nurturing when one's own needs for nurture are still strong, makes the formation of a consistent, whole, and meaningful definition of self difficult if not impossible to attain. Unfortunately, the social and cultural conditions that give rise to teenage pregnancy are not easily remedied. This is particularly true today when so many supports for sexual restraint are missing and when encouragement for engaging in sexual activity is present everywhere. Sex education will not help the situation as long as every other avenue of information geared to the teenager (books, movies, TV, music lyrics, advertising) proclaims the "joy of sex."

We have now looked at some of the permutations that characterize contemporary American family life. We have also seen that such permutations are perhaps hardest upon teenagers. The family is in flux just when the young person is trying to discover what is constant in his or her self-definition and what this means for being a man or a woman, a husband or a wife, a father or a mother. When the people who have filled those roles in the past and who have been the primary models for them suddenly change their behavior and allegiances, the basic ground on which teenagers form their identity is shaken as if by an earthquake. If parents consider the needs of their teenagers, as well as their own, some of the stress of family permutations can be lessened, if not avoided.

Chapter 7

Schools for Scandal

A school for Scandal! tell me, I beseech you
Needs there a school this modish art to teach you?
No need of lessons now, the knowing think;
We might as well be taught to eat and drink.[1]

Richard Brinsley Sheridan's play *The School for Scandal*, first produced in 1777, was a comedy of manners and a light satire on the time and energy the upper classes of that era spent on gossip and innuendo. In our day, the American high school has become a school for scandal in a literal sense. As at least a half-dozen recent reports make clear, the majority of high schools in this country are doing a poor job of educating teenagers.[2] A less publicized but more serious scandal is the failure of our schools to provide teenagers with a protected place in which they can get on with the task of building an identity.

The fault, of course, cannot be laid entirely on the schools. Our schools in large measure reflect the values, tensions, and stresses of the larger society. Nevertheless, in a very real sense, our schools do fail to provide for the educational and personal identity needs of teenagers. The facts are ominous. Falling SAT scores, poor showings on achievement tests in comparison with the young from other countries, widespread violence, drug abuse, and crime on high school campuses—these constitute the scandal of our schools. Some of the dimensions of this scandal are shown by the following statistics reported in the 1983 report of the National Commission on Excellence in Education.

> International comparisons of student achievement completed a decade ago reveal that on 19 academic tests, American students were never first or second and, in comparison with students from other industrialized nations, were last seven times.

> The College Board's scholastic aptitude tests (SATs) demonstrate a virtually unbroken decline from 1963 to 1980. Average verbal scores fell over 50 points and average mathematics scores nearly 40 points.

> Many 17 year olds do not possess the "higher order" intellectual skills we should expect of them. Nearly 40 percent cannot draw inferences from written material; only one-fifth can write a persuasive essay; and only one-third can solve a mathematics problem requiring several steps.[3]

These statistics and those reported in other publications on this issue paint a disturbing picture of the decline in the academic standards and abilities of young Americans.

The other, less publicized, scandal of our schools is their failure to provide a protected place for teenagers to struggle with the difficult task of growing up. The high school was once a special place for teenagers; it was in fact "their" place. It was a place where they could devote their energies to the task of personal, social, and occupational growth without pressure from the "real world." It was a place where the teenager was safe. It was, as Ernest Boyer wrote, "the one institution where it is all right to be young."[4]

Unfortunately, it is no longer all right to be young in today's schools, where the prevalence of drugs, sex, and violence makes youthful vulnerability a handicap. As one writer explains:

> Drugs, for an enormous number of kids, are not merely a weekend enterprise; many of them get high or drunk during the day, during class. High school teachers, even in comfortable suburban school districts, often describe their work as being more like that of a traffic cop than an educator: "I keep them in line until the three o'clock bell," one former student of mine recently told me. "A good day is one in which nobody gets freaky."[5]

This type of description, now fairly common, does not present the vision of a safe and secure place of learning.

The very same transformations of the American high school that have produced the scandal of academic underachievement have also produced the less well-known scandal of personal underachievement, a result of the contemporary teenager's low self-esteem. The transformations responsible for both scandals were the change from small school to big school, from a fixed menu to a smorgasbord curriculum, and, finally, from the joy of teaching to the chore of teaching. To understand how these changes came about, we must first review the history of the American high school in general.

History of the American High School

Like Harvard, Boston tends to be first or last in any number of things. The English Classical School, the first public high school in the United States, opened its doors in Boston in 1821. According to Ernest Boyer in his book, *Highschool*,

> The English Classical School—whose name was shortened to English High School—admitted only students twelve years of age or older, boys from mercantile or mechanical classes (families) who were well acquainted with reading, writing, English grammar in all of its branches and arithmetic. These

139

young men pursued a three year course of study in compo-
sition, declamation, mathematics, history, civics, logic, sur-
veying, navigation, and moral and political philosophy.[6]

But it was not until 1874, when the Michigan State Supreme Court ruled that taxes could be levied to support public
high schools as well as elementary schools, that the American
high school began to take firm root. With urbanization, mag-
nificent high schools were constructed in some of the largest
cities in the nation—San Francisco, New York and St. Louis.
These public high schools could compare with the best of the
private academies regardless of their tradition and prestige.
Many urban high schools also graduated young women trained
in normal classes to become teachers.[7]

Since the beginning of the present century, the building
of new high schools and high school enrollments have increased at a steady pace. At the turn of the century there were
about six thousand high schools in the United States, and these
served 519,000 students. At the time, this number of students
represented only 8.5 percent of the total youth population. It
should be said, too, that not all the young people who attended
high school graduated in those days. Only about 75 percent of
the students attending high school completed their studies.

The progress in public education since the turn of the century is made clear by the following statistics. The recent census
(1981) indicates that today some 94.1 percent of all the young
people from fourteen to seventeen years of age in this country
are attending junior or senior high school. In actual numbers
this means that about 13.5 million teenagers are enrolled in
junior and senior high schools today. Since 1970, the percentage
of teenagers who actually graduate from high school has been
about 75 percent (which means that the dropout rate today is
roughly what it was eighty years ago, when a much smaller
proportion of the youth population was in school).[8]

At the present time, therefore, almost all the teenagers in
this country spend at least part of their teen years in school.
Although universal high school education is an accomplishment of which we can be proud, the declining academic

achievement of teenagers and their diminished success at acquiring a healthy sense of identity are scandals that we can ill afford. We need now to look in more detail at each of the transformations the high school has undergone in this century and what they have done to teenagers' efforts to achieve a clear definition of themselves.

The Big School

American schools started out as rather small enterprises, but over the last forty years the trend has been toward bigness in everything, including schools. Large schools, unfortunately, make it more difficult for young people to construct their identity. The change in the size of American schools is vividly described by Diane Ravitch in *The Troubled Crusade*:

> Beyond the obvious gains and losses that had been registered in the course of thirty-five years was a change in climate so basic and yet so elusive that it was difficult to measure or even describe. Although some few big city high schools were vast educational factories in 1945, most schools, colleges, and even universities were small compared to what was to come. In some communities, teachers "boarded" with families, not because of choice but because of low pay; not a situation they might have chosen, but one that assured intimate familiarity with the community and the children. Even where teachers led independent lives, they were expected to spend after-school hours as supervisors of extracurricular activities and to know their students; they in turn could count on parents to support and reinforce the demands made by the school. Colleges and universities never questioned their role *in loco parentis*: they were responsible for the young men and women in their care, as if the institution itself were their parents. Alcohol was seldom permitted on campus, drugs were unheard of, and even the social lives of students were regulated; infractions of the rules of behavior might be punished by suspension or expulsion.[9]

141

Most adults today will recognize some of the features of the small school as part of their school experience. Ravitch then contrasts this picture with the educational scene in 1980:

> Much had changed by 1980. The drive to consolidate small schools and small school districts had largely succeeded, helped along by the vast expansion of enrollments in the 1950's and 1960's. Big schools became the rule, not the exception. In a society where bigger was considered better, small districts and small schools were described as backward and inefficient. The number of school districts shrank dramatically, from one hundred thousand at war's end to sixteen thousand in 1980. While total enrollment in elementary and secondary school nearly doubled during the 35 year span (from 23 million to 40 million), the number of schools dropped from one hundred and eighty-five thousand to eighty-six thousand. More and more students went to larger schools. In higher education, institutions enrolling more than twenty thousand students increased from ten in 1948 to one hundred and fifteen by 1980. Growth had many benefits: efficiency of scale, diversity of curriculum, differentiation of types of students and teachers. Enlargement meant exposure to a more varied setting and interaction with a broader variety of ideas and people than was possible in a small school or college.[10]

Although bigness has certain economic and administrative advantages, its disadvantages for schools are only now beginning to be recognized. Again, Ravitch makes the case:

> The trade off, of course, was that bigness meant impersonality, bureaucratization, diminished contact between faculty and students, formalization of relationships among colleagues, a weakening of the bonds of community. Colleges and universities withdrew from the *in loco parentis* role that they had previously exercised. No longer part of a community of values shared with students and parents, teachers and administrators found it difficult to administer discipline or even to establish rules that everyone found acceptable. Teachers and professors defended themselves against the new anonymity by joining unions. Students, complaining that no

one knew their names, wrote them vividly in the bathrooms and hallways of their schools. The invasion of drugs, first in college in the 1960's then in the high schools and even junior highs in the 1970's, dulled students' senses and insulated a portion of the student body from adult standards. The lingering influence of the counterculture, that remnant of the 1960's youth rebellion, left many adults wondering whether there were any standards of learning or effort or behavior worth defending.[11]

From a small, orderly world of knowns, certainties, and reasonable expectations students have entered a world of unknowns, uncertainties, confusions, and often danger.

What does large school size and large class size mean from the standpoint of the teenager's efforts at self-definition? One clear consequence is the loss of what has been called *mentoring*. In the autobiographies of many men and women who became successful despite adversity, one repeatedly finds that a significant person in their lives recognized their special gifts and devoted time, energy, and skill to helping them realize their abilities. More often than not, this significant person was a teacher or coach whom the successful person first encountered in school. Although teacher and pupil did not meet at school, the importance of the role of the mentor is best illustrated by the case of Helen Keller. As a young child she was not only deaf and blind but nearly demented in her behavior. It took the insight, dedication, and hard work of her teacher, Anne Sullivan, to enable Helen Keller to realize her intellectual and artistic gifts. The establishment of a mentor relationship is much more likely in the small high school, with its small classes, than in the large high school. It is next to impossible, for example, for an English teacher who sees two hundred students a day to single out a few to work with intensively. Many gifted and talented students fail to realize their potential because the bigness of today's schools militates against the mentoring of such students by individual faculty members.

School size affects teenagers' efforts to define themselves in still other ways. Self-definition, for example, is facilitated by being with people who know us well and who give us useful information about ourselves. The more people who know us well, the more likely we are to get a balanced picture of ourselves, since the biases of one person will more than likely cancel out those of another. In large schools teenagers know, and are known by, fewer people than would be the case in small schools. The difference between the two types of schools is a little like the difference between a small town and a big one. In a small town everyone is likely to know everyone else, whereas in a big town most people are strangers to each other. For an adult, one who has a well-defined sense of self, the anonymity of a large city may be welcome since it allows the individual to live life in his or her own way. But for a young person who is just attaining an identity, the evaluations and responses of a variety of different people who really know him or her contribute to a solidly grounded identity. Within a large circle of friends and acquaintances, the teenager comes to understand how he or she is both the same as and different from others. In a large school the teenager is deprived of this variety of input about himself or herself.

It is also true, as Ravitch suggested in the passage cited earlier, that bigness contributes to the prevalence of substance abuse, theft, vandalism, and violence in the high schools. Social controls are weaker in large schools than in small schools, just as they are weaker in large cities than in small cities. The importance of social controls is demonstrated by the behavior of conventioneers in a strange city. When they are in a city where they are not known, people will sometimes do things that they would never do at home. The same is true for students in large high schools, regardless of where the high school is located—in city or country. The large rural "comprehensive" high schools that draw students from several surrounding small towns may create a big-city atmosphere. In such schools young people may feel free to do things they would never dare do in their home communities. The result is that the rural comprehensive high school leads to the same problems as those that prevail in large urban high schools.

We should not make the mistake of assuming that, like conventioneers, teenagers want the opportunity to act in an environment free of the usual constraints. For young people in the process of constructing a conception of themselves and the world, the lawlessness of the large school can be alarming. Seeing other young people breaking the rules with impunity forces teenagers to question the rules they have been taught and their own system of personal values. As an illustration, here are the remarks of a twelfth-grader attending an inner-city high school who was asked to give a reason for hating school:

> There are only one or two reasons why I hate school. One of them is because of all the racial incidents in our school system. For example, in our last school year one student was walking down the third floor corridor. He was the only one of his color who was on the floor at the time.
> He was beaten very badly. . . . Nothing was heard of this. I'm sure someone took the blame for it but no one ever heard about it. When no one knows if or if not the students were punished they automatically think they can do it and get away with it . . . something must be done.[12]

As we listen to the student, we hear more than that he disapproved of the racist attack; his sense of personal justice was offended. He expected the adults in charge of the school to find the culprits, announce the proper punishment, and carry it out. Clearly this is not what happened, and it upset this teenager's value system. The questioning brought on by such experiences may be healthy for those young people who already have a strong sense of who and what they are. For teenagers who have already attained a strong identity, such experiences help them further differentiate themselves from the kind of hoodlum who would engage in such attacks. For teenagers who have not yet attained a strong sense of their own self and identity, that kind of an experience may have the opposite effect. In such young people the experience can lead to the conclusion that anything goes and you can get away with anything if you are clever. They learn, not the difference between right and wrong, but what you can and cannot get away with. This amounts to growth by substitution, because the young person learns to look to the particular situation for guides to action rather than to fixed inner standards that can serve in many different situations.

The Smorgasbord Curriculum

An integrated course of study at the junior and senior high school levels can promote integrated personal as well as intellectual growth. Unfortunately, the high school curriculum has become increasingly fragmented over the last few decades. This process was accelerated after 1965 and the entrance of the federal government into educational policy making. To meet the needs of all young people, the schools developed special programs for disadvantaged youth, for handicapped youth, for bilingual youth, and for gifted and talented young people, and they introduced courses in drug education, sex education, moral development, values clarification and problem solving, the Holocaust, nuclear war, and so on.

The schools have done extraordinarily well in meeting these diverse special needs, but in the process of doing so the curriculum has lost its focus. The aim of education—to provide young people with the basic skills, the fundamental knowledge, and the human values that will enable them both to realize themselves and to become productive, responsible citizens—has become enmeshed in a net of special interests. To be sure, meeting the needs of these groups was long overdue. Even so, these needs are too often being met at the expense of the needs common to all teenagers. All teenagers, whether handicapped or not, whether disadvantaged or not, whether bilingual or not, whether gifted or not, whether average or not, are trying to construct an integrated definition of who they are and a healthy sense of personal identity. An integrated curriculum of skills, knowledge, and values provides the teenager with a model for constructing an integrated self of specific social skills, social knowledge, and values.

Too often, special programs and courses emphasize the differences among teenagers rather than their similarities. By focusing on the adjective (retarded, gifted, handicapped) rather than the noun (the teenager), such courses and programs miss the student, who is first and foremost a young person. Programs that single out special groups and label them may help a teenager achieve self-definition in a negative way, by forcing that teenager to accept a definition of who he or she is that separates him or her from friends and peers. Such special programs also serve to fragment the curriculum and deny special-needs students the benefits to be derived from participating in an integrated course of study.

Before we consider in detail how the smorgasbord curriculum hinders self-differentiation, we need to examine how it came to be. As the public high school movement became a national reality, a battle over the curriculum erupted, and it has continued with more or less the same intensity until the present day. On the one hand were those who believed that all students should be prepared in the same way, regardless of their future vocation. For example, at the turn of the century a blue ribbon commission called the Committee of Ten and headed by Charles W. Eliot (then president of Harvard) argued for a curriculum that encouraged "mental discipline." This mental discipline, it was asserted, came from learning certain subjects, namely, Latin, Greek, and higher mathematics.

According to this commission, students should prepare for work in the same way they prepare for college, on the premise that mental discipline, like self-discipline, is required in all walks of life and for all vocations. Furthermore, this form of education opened the door of opportunity equally wide for all students. Charles Eliot wrote that he staunchly refused to believe "that the American public intends to have its children sorted before their teens into clerks, watchmakers, lithographers, telegraph operators, masons, teamsters, farm laborers, and so forth, and treated differently in their schools according to these prophecies of their appropriate life careers. Who are we to make these prophecies? Can parents? Can teachers?"[13]

The opposing camp asserted that the subjects taught in high school should be applicable to "real life." This clearly eliminated those courses (such as Latin and Greek) that were supposed to encourage mental discipline but that did not have, or at least did not appear to have, much practical utility. Such was the position, for example, of those involved in what has come to be called the "progressive education" movement, which virtually dominated the educational scene during the 1930s and 1940s. This position was epitomized by Charles Prosser, who wrote in 1939:

> On all these counts, business arithmetic is superior to plane or solid geometry; learning ways of keeping physically fit, to the study of French; learning the techniques of selecting an occupation, to the study of algebra; simple science of everyday life, to geology; simple business English, to Elizabethan Classics.[14]

The battle between these two camps continues today, between those who advocate a core curriculum and those who advocate what is called social relevance. The launching of *Sputnik* in 1956, for example, set off a whole new set of investigations, reports, and initiatives on the improvement of American education. In his 1959 report on American schools, James B. Conant, then president of Harvard, advocated not only school consolidation but also a return to a core curriculum of "hard" subjects—mathematics, science, and foreign languages.[15] *Sputnik* gave impetus to the federal government's involvement in education and the initiation of several curriculum projects (including the new math) sponsored by federal agencies such as the National Science Foundation.

The progress toward a solid core curriculum of hard subjects was short-lived, however, to some degree because of the failure of the new curriculums but even more because of the social upheavals of the 1960s, the civil rights movement, the women's movement, and the Vietnam War. These events brought forth a new group of people concerned about education who advocated a curriculum with more practical utility. As Boyer points out, the times created "a new group of reformers, including James Coleman and John Henry Martin, who argued that the road of relevance was beyond the school. Educators were urged to provide more real life experiences for the young—work study programs, 'action learning,' cities-as-schools, and the like."[16]

In the late seventies and early eighties, American society has again leaned toward the conservative side, and this is reflected in its current educational trend. The "back to basics" movement is a return to the idea of the core curriculum and to a focus on the common needs of all students. As famed educator Robert Maynard Hutchins put it, "The best education for the best," he said, "is the best education for all."[17]

The result of this ongoing battle is that most high schools today have some combination of the two approaches, and in the majority of schools, the goal of social relevance seems to carry more weight than the standard, or core, curriculum. This is the conclusion reached recently by the National Commission on Excellence in Education:

> Secondary school curricula have been homogenized, diluted and diffused to the point that they no longer have a central purpose. In effect we have a cafeteria style curriculum in which the appetizers and desserts can easily be mistaken for the main courses. Students have migrated from vocational and college preparatory courses to general track courses in large numbers. The proportion of students taking a general course of study has increased from 12 percent in 1964 to 42 percent in 1979.
>
> The curricular smorgasbord, combined with extensive student choice, explains a great deal about where we find ourselves today. We offer intermediate algebra, but only 31 percent of our recent high school graduates complete it; we offer French I, but only 13 percent complete it; and we offer geography, but only 16 percent complete it. Calculus is avail-

able in schools enrolling about 60 percent of all students, but only 6 percent complete it.

Twenty-five percent of the credits earned by general track high school students are in physical and health education, work experiences outside the school, remedial English and mathematics, and personal service and development courses such as training for adulthood and marriage.[18]

Whatever the merits of one course of study over another, students have clearly chosen the smorgasbord approach.

From the standpoint of self-differentiation and identity formation, the contemporary high school curriculum has two negative effects. One of them derives from the smorgasbord component of the curriculum and the other derives from the core component. A healthy sense of self and identity is acquired by differentiation and higher-order integration. An integrated curriculum fosters such growth at both the personal and the intellectual level, and this is why it has been advocated by educators such as Eliot, Conant, and Hutchins who are concerned with the whole student rather than with one particular skill or area bit of knowledge. When a student learns something in one class that sheds light on another, when he or she realizes what a scientific discovery, for instance, did to the political thinking of an era, there is growth by differentiation and integration. Such learning adds not only to young people's sense of intellectual integration but also to their sense of personal integration. That learning becomes their knowledge, something they possess and can advance or utilize as they choose.

A smorgasbord curriculum, in contrast, has obvious disadvantages from the standpoint of defining a personal identity. Studies that do not relate in any way to each other—sex education to algebra, for example—are likely to foster growth by substitution both intellectually and personally. Knowledge is kept in separate categories that cannot be related or brought together. This gives rise to a kind of compartmentalization of thinking about the self as well. What the young person learns about himself or herself in one situation is not extended or carried over to new and different situations because the new situations are too different from the original learning situation. Often, such a curriculum turns the student off to learning, period. Consider the following fictional but all-too-common reaction of a student in a social studies class:

> (Teacher) What parties am I talking about?
> Listen to your stomach growl. Hope that nobody hears.
> Do not look around. Put head down on desk and go to sleep.
> Clean nails with the point of a compass. Drop comb on floor;
> retrieve it with your foot.[19]

A smorgasbord curriculum, therefore, discourages growth by integration both intellectually and personally.

The core curriculum presents its own barriers to self-differentiation. Ironically, the benefits of a core curriculum are considerable for a student with formal operations, but they may not be accessible to a student who has not yet attained the ability to think in a new key. Many high school subjects, such as algebra, require formal operations to be fully understood and appreciated. The same is true for experimental science, history, and literature. These subjects cannot serve the purpose of mental discipline if they are beyond the student's comprehension in the first place. Many students fail or are turned off by the core curriculum subjects, not because they are lazy or dull or interested in other things, but because they cannot really understand what is going on and find the experience frustrating. The age at which young people attain formal operations can vary as much as the age at which they attain puberty. Teenagers of the same chronological age in junior high school may be at quite different levels of mental development.

Consider what this means for a young person's evolving sense of self. Computer courses are a case in point. Learning and fully understanding computer programming and computer languages such as BASIC, Pascal, or FORTRAN require formal operations. It makes sense, therefore, to teach programming at the higher grades—tenth, eleventh, and twelfth—when most students have probably attained formal operations. But suppose a young man or woman who has not yet attained formal operations takes a course in computer programming and discovers that he or she can't figure out what is going on. In most cases the student will not blame the teacher or the text or his or her enrollment in the course. More often these students will blame themselves and incorporate the notion that they cannot understand computers into their definition of themselves. Given today's world, such a self-perception can be a serious vocational and emotional handicap.

Learning computer programming should be compared to learning Greek and Latin. Few students, unless they become programmers, are going to use their programming skills, any more than they will the dead languages. Nevertheless, a knowledge of Latin gives us a deeper and clearer sense of the English language and of history and culture than we would have achieved without it. Learning Latin helps students to further distinguish themselves as speakers of a particular type of language and to integrate their knowledge with that of the world. Knowing a computer language has the same differentiating and integrating effect. The teenager who knows one or more computer languages is in a good position to understand the application of computers in many different fields. At the same time, these skills add to the teenager's sense of competence and self-esteem.

If learning computer languages is understood as analogous to learning dead languages, then we will have put it in the right perspective. Students do not need to learn programming in order to use computers any more than they need to learn Latin to use English. But learning programming can be put in the service of mental discipline and as such should find a place in the core curriculum, provided that students who take the course have attained formal operations. Unfortunately, this is often not done, and programming is taught too early and for the wrong reasons, with disastrous consequences for many young people.

The Chore of Teaching

Teachers are important role models for students. When teachers are no longer excited about what they are teaching and have lost their commitment to young people, their effectiveness as role models is diminished or lost. Although there were always some teachers who were in education for the wrong reasons, there were always enough dedicated teachers to maintain the balance and give students someone they could look up to, admire, and emulate. For this reason, much healthy self-differentiation and identity formation can occur within the context of the teacher-student relationship. Yet the climate necessary to foster good teaching in the modern high school has virtually disappeared. Even dedicated teachers are becoming discouraged, as this one explains:

> I'm not receiving the same positive response from my students. In the past, I felt more like a coach to my students, helping them achieve the highest level of skills they're capable of. But I've felt more in an adversarial position recently and I don't know why. It's almost as if they say, "I defy you to teach me." I had one class of students last year with a dozen chronic behavior problems. I dreaded dealing with that class every day. It affected my whole life.[20]

Another teacher, with twenty years of experience, put it this way:

> When you accept the role of being a teacher, your satisfaction comes when you know you've helped and served. Satisfaction in teaching is having a student come back saying, "I learned something." Being around young people is a reward in itself. But those rewards are getting fewer. . . . My major problem is how to motivate students who don't care about themselves. Any my biggest frustration is their "What's the difference?" attitude. Those who do care seem to be dwindling every year. You know how many kids ever come back to say "thanks"?[21]

What has taken the joy out of teaching and made it such a chore? The causes are as many and varied as they are familiar. Thanks to the family permutations and vanishing markers of the place of teenagers in today's society, many more students than ever before are troubled, unhappy, and difficult to reach. In addition, as schools have grown larger and become more bureaucratized and more subject to government regulation, the amount of paperwork and record keeping has increased tremendously. Salaries have not kept pace with the rate of inflation in the economy, and the always ambivalent attitude of the larger society toward teachers has become increasingly one-sided and negative. As Boyer writes in his book, *Highschool*:

> Today, teaching occupies an even more "shadowed place" in the public's esteem. In just twelve years, from 1969 to 1981, the number of parents who said they would like to have their children become teachers in the public schools dropped from 75 to 46 percent. Seventy-one percent of the senior high school teachers sampled in another survey indicated that public attitudes toward schools had a negative effect on their job satisfaction. And a science teacher who left the profession in disgust after twenty years told us that if his daughter elects teaching as a profession he will not pay for her education.[22]

When teaching becomes a chore, as it has for all too many teachers today, this has a twofold impact on instruction: standards are lowered and requirements are reduced. Both of these changes militate against healthy intellectual and identity development in the teenager. We have already seen what the decline in educational standards has done to the academic achievement of teenagers: the enormous drop in SAT scores over the last two decades is testimony to the negative effect of declining standards on academic achievement.

But what does this decline in standards do to young people's sense of self and identity when they are not challenged to do their best and are allowed to get away with sloppy work, with not handing in assignments, with not doing the required reading?

The standards we set for ourselves are initially the standards that others set for us, which eventually become our own. Students who are never really challenged, never really forced to stretch themselves, never really prodded to the self-discipline of doing necessary work when it needs to be done, miss an important opportunity to learn more about themselves, about what they are truly capable of doing. If a high school student can get along with the same loose work habits established in elementary or junior high school, he or she has not really profited from the educational experience, either intellectually or personally. A precious opportunity has been lost beyond recovery.

That teaching is now a chore is also manifest in the reduced requirements placed on students. This is particularly true in the realm of homework. Almost every recent study of high schools has made a point of advocating more homework. For example, a study of high schools by James Coleman reported that in high-performance high schools (those in which students performed at high levels on academic tests) more homework was assigned than in low-performance schools.[23] Nevertheless, it is a mistake to attribute the benefits of homework solely to its self-disciplinary effects; we must also consider its interpersonal value.

This, unfortunately, is where Amitai Etzioni, a well-known educational sociologist, errs in his response to the Coleman findings. Etzioni says, "Homework is an important measure of self discipline because students must do it on a regular basis and without close supervision."[24] This interpretation suggests that homework is valuable in itself, regardless of how or when it is corrected or responded to. But that is hardly the case. Homework provides an opportunity for close, personal, and private interaction between student and teacher. For this reason it is important for teenagers: it is precisely the kind of interaction they are seeking in their efforts at self-definition. Young people take homework assignments seriously, at least at first, because they assume the teacher will take them seriously too. If the teacher reads the student's work carefully and responds to it honestly, it is tremendously rewarding to the teenager.

Not the least of its value is the affirmation such a response provides for the young person's sense of self-esteem and personal worth.

On the other hand, when teachers are too busy and too overwhelmed to give much homework, or too overworked to give it their attention, the results are predictable. If little or no homework is given, the student attributes this to the teacher's indifference or laziness. If the homework is required but is not returned immediately with many comments, the student is upset. It does not matter that the homework was turned in late, that it was almost illegible, and that it had not been given the same time or attention the student demanded of the teacher.

When teachers have the time and energy to correct homework, they have an opportunity to establish a positive, constructive relationship with a willing partner, and they can begin to correct some of the student attitudes and behaviors previously described. That is the beauty of homework—it provides a useful arena for social learning. But if teachers cannot do their jobs, they are in no position to make demands upon the student. Nothing positive will be achieved by simply assigning more homework for students if teachers are not given the time and institutional support they need to make the homework worthwhile.

Part III

Result:
Stress and
Its Aftermath

Chapter 8

Stress, Identity, and the Patchwork Self

Stress is a basic fact of our lives, and how we learn to deal with it in adolescence will determine how well we handle it in our later years. How does stress work? What are its energy dynamics? And how does an integrated sense of identity enable us to manage stress efficiently? These are questions we have to answer before we can grasp why a patchwork self, in its many different forms, does the opposite—namely, mismanages stress.

The Stress Reaction

Stress is always an excessive demand for adjustment. As living organisms, we must constantly respond to inner and outer demands for adaptation. Some of these inner and outer demands are biological and specific, such as hunger, thirst, and the need to keep warm in freezing temperatures. Other inner and outer demands are psychological but equally specific, such as the demands made upon us by traffic signals and alarm clocks, or our need for mental challenge or mental relaxation. Our reactions to these demands are well matched. We eat when we are hungry, drink when we are thirsty, and add clothing when the temperature goes down. Our reactions to particular psychological demands are also well suited. We stop at red lights and get out of bed more or less quickly after the alarm goes off. Likewise, we may read a book or do a crossword puzzle for mental challenge or watch television for mental relaxation.

There are other demands, however, that are more powerful and pressing than those described above. If we are exposed to extreme cold or to extreme heat or if we are forced to go without food or water for any length of time, habitual reactions will not suffice to remedy the situation. Similarly, many psychological demands are much more powerful than those described above. If we lose our job or get passed over for a promotion or win a much-coveted honor, the demands for adjustment are powerful indeed. These sometimes abrupt, always powerful pressures for action are what we mean when we speak of *stress*: an excessive demand for adjustment that can arise from within or from outside of ourselves.

Unlike our very specific reactions to the moderate demands made upon us, our response to stress, regardless of its nature or origin, is always the same. This was the discovery of Hans Selye, the physiologist who first introduced the concept of stress and who has initiated the scientific study of this reaction.[1] Selye has labeled this common pattern of reaction to excessive demands for action the General Adaptation Syndrome (GAS). According to Selye, whenever we are confronted with a stress situation, a general physiological mobilization of our bodies occurs.

This physiological stress reaction has two stages. The first is the shock stage, which reflects our initial reaction to a severe, unexpected demand for action. Signs of injury appear: heartbeat is irregular, blood pressure falls, muscle tone is lost, and body temperature drops. Then, in the countershock stage, the body reactions are reversed and prepare us for defense. The adrenal cortex is mobilized and enlarged, and the production of corticoid hormones is stimulated. Now heart rate and blood pressure increase, as does body temperature. Muscle tone is restored, and we are prepared for either "fight or flight."

Our psychological reaction to stress follows a parallel course.

When we first hear bad news or good news, we are stunned, not really able to take in the information that has been revealed to us. After the initial shock of disbelief, the defense reaction follows. If we failed to get a much-desired promotion, we may rationalize that it would entail too much work anyway or deny that we really wanted it or blame the decision on politics and the successful candidate's strategy of playing up to the boss. If the news is good, we reassess ourselves and the boss in a new and more favorable light. In victory, we may even be gracious to the unsuccessful candidate.

The way our bodies and minds mobilize for action in response to excessive demands of any kind is clearly a carryover from our evolutionary heritage as hunters and gatherers in the wild. Such mobilization was essential if human beings were to survive in a world where most of the dangers came from without and were difficult, if not impossible, to anticipate and to prepare for. For most people today, however, the body mobilizes its defenses in response to psychological rather than physical danger. And psychological stress, since it comes from ourselves or from other people, is in many cases foreseeable. We humans tend to operate in habitual and predictable ways. Accordingly, although we are still subject to stress in today's world, we are also in a better position to manage it.

Stress management is very important. In modern society we can rarely take refuge in the physical action that the stress response prepares us for. In many cases, the mobilized energy is discharged through one or another body organ, and we experience a stress symptom such as headache, stomachache, or nervous tension. If the stress continues and we have no other outlet, chronic stress diseases may result, such as migraine, ulcers, or colitis.

Psychological stress affects not only the body but also our quality of life. The quality of our lives depends upon how much energy we have to devote to the various types of activities that add up to a satisfying life-style. If much of our available energy is burned up in stress reactions, there will be less for other activities. If we are always dealing with crises, our leisure is spent recuperating and there is no time to take genuine pleasure in life. Stress burns energy, and to see how it affects our lives we have to look at its energy dynamics.

Stress Dynamics

As biological organisms, we run on two different but related kinds of energy. One of these might be called *clock* energy. This is the energy that we burn up in any twenty-four-hour period and that is replenishable with food and rest. It is the energy we use for our ordinary activities. A second type of energy might be called *calendar* energy. Unlike clock energy, calendar energy comes to us in more or less fixed amounts, is determined by our genetic endowment, and is not replenishable. Calendar energy is generally used for growth and development. Although our daily fund of clock energy tends to decline with age, the decline tends to be gradual and to be compensated by more efficient budgeting of time and effort. Calendar energy, since it is concerned with growth, is apportioned unequally at different stages in the life cycle. Children and teenagers, for example, use proportionately more energy for the purpose of growing than adults. Although growth occurs at every stage of life, far more occurs in the early years, and therefore far more calendar energy is required during those years. Making so much of our calendar energy available to us when we are children and teenagers may be nature's way of supporting the laborious and energy-consuming process of constructing an integrated sense of self and identity. But, as we shall see, when this energy is well invested, it pays rich dividends later.

To better understand the relationship between the two kinds of energy, we can think of clock energy as the money we have in our checking account and of calendar energy as the money in our savings account. In general, we try to meet our recurring weekly and monthly expenses out of our checking accounts, which we regularly replenish with deposits from our weekly or monthly salaries or the profit from our business or professional fees. Our savings accounts, in contrast, are usually re-

162

served for major purchases such as a house, a car, our children's college education, and, eventually, our retirement.

How we manage our checking and savings accounts reflects on our style of life. If we repeatedly overspend our checking accounts—by buying expensive clothing, stereo equipment, or other luxury items that we really cannot afford—we eventually have to draw upon our savings accounts. As a consequence we jeopardize our long-term goals for short-term pleasures. On the other hand, if we are so concerned with putting away money for the future that we are reluctant to indulge in any extravagance—even to the extent of not going out to dinner on occasion or once in a while buying something we like but really could do without—the quality of our daily life suffers at the expense of our long-range plans. The goal we all work toward is to have an enjoyable life day to day while still putting enough away so that our future needs will be comfortably looked after.

In the same way, how we manage our reserves of energy also reflects upon the quality of our lives. Suppose, for example, that our everyday lives are full of stress. We work with and for people whom we neither like nor respect, and this makes demands upon us over and above the demands of our work. If, in addition, we have a stressful home life that absorbs more than the usual amount of energy, we will necessarily overexpend our clock energy and be forced to draw upon our calendar energy.

The consequences are twofold. Biologically, the continual mobilization of the body for fight or flight can produce diseases related to chronic stress and/or premature aging. Psychologically, the drain on our long-term reserves reduces the amount of calendar energy that we will have available to meet the demands of our later growth phases, such as midlife crises. If we do not have the energy necessary to deal with these later periods, we may succumb to disease or to psychological arrest. A case in point is the person who, five years after getting a divorce, still insists that things are as they were with his or her former spouse.

It is important to recognize that the stress that saps one's reserves may come from within as well as from without. The individual who did not complete the process of constructing a sense of self and identity as an adolescent may persist in this quest as an adult. In this type of individual, energy that might be spent in the joys of everyday life, in the pleasures of family, work, and recreation, is spent instead upon what seems an unending quest for self-definition. Such persons are the neurotics of our time. Totally self-centered, they look at each new situation as an opportunity to learn something about themselves. Sometimes charming, sometimes annoying, always demanding, they are at best tolerated by friends and family. Their lack of development leaves them isolated and out of phase with everyone who has completed the process.

Again, the goal we need to work for is to manage our energy budget in such a way that we can live an enjoyable daily life and still have abundant energy for further personal growth and development. How, then, does the construction of an integrated sense of self and identity move us toward this goal?

Stress and Identity

Most situations that produce psychological stress involve some sort of conflict between self and society. So long as we satisfy a social demand at the expense of a personal need, or vice versa, the social or personal demand for action is a psychological stress. If, for example, we stay home from work because of a personal problem, we create a new demand (for an explanation, for made-up time) at our place of work. On the other hand, if we devote too much time to the demands of work, we create new demands on the part of family. If we don't manage our energy budgets well, we create more stress than is necessary.

The major task of psychological stress management is to find ways to balance and coordinate the demands that come from within with those that come from without. This is where a healthy sense of self and identity comes in. An integrated sense of identity, as we have seen, means bringing together into a working whole a set of attitudes, values, and habits that

164

can serve both self and society. The attainment of such a sense of identity is accompanied by a feeling of self-esteem, of liking and respecting oneself and being liked and respected by others.

More than anything else, the attainment of a healthy sense of identity and a feeling of self-esteem gives young people a perspective, a way of looking at themselves and others, which enables them to manage the majority of stress situations. Young people with high self-esteem look at situations from a single perspective that includes both themselves and others. They look at situations from the standpoint of what it means to their self-respect and to the respect others have for them. This integrated perspective enables them to manage the major types of stress efficiently and with a minimum expenditure of energy and personal distress.

The Three Stress Situations

There are three major types of stress situation that all of us encounter. One of these occurs when the potential stress is both foreseeable and avoidable. This is a *Type A* stress situation. If we are thinking about going on a roller coaster or seeing a horror movie, the stress is both foreseeable and avoidable. We may choose to expose ourselves to the stress if we find such controlled danger situations exciting or stimulating. Likewise if we know that a particular neighborhood or park is dangerous at night, the danger is both foreseeable and avoidable, and we do avoid it, unless we are looking for trouble.

The situation becomes more complicated when the foreseeable and avoidable danger is one for which there is much social approval and support, even though it entails much personal risk. Becoming a soldier in times of war is an example of this more complicated Type A danger. The young person who enlists wins social approval at the risk of personal harm. On the other hand, the young person who refuses to become a soldier protects himself or herself from danger at the cost of social disapproval.

Teenagers are often caught in this more difficult type of

situation. If the peer group uses alcohol or drugs, for example, there is considerable pressure on the young person to participate. But such participation often puts the teenager at risk with parents and teachers, and also with respect to themselves. They may not like the image of themselves as drinkers or drug abusers. It is at this point that a sense of identity and a positive feeling of self-esteem stand the teenager in good stead.

A young person with a healthy sense of identity will weigh the danger to his or her hard-won feeling of self-esteem against the feelings associated with the loss of peer approval. When the teenager looks at the situation from this perspective, the choice is easy to make. By weighing the laboriously arrived-at feeling of self-esteem against the momentary approval of a transient peer group, the teenager with an integrated sense of self is able to avoid potentially stressful situations. It should be said, too, that the young person's ability to foresee and avoid is both an intellectual and an emotional achievement. The teenager must be able to foresee events (made possible in part by thinking in a new key) but also to place sufficient value upon his or her self-esteem and self-respect to avoid situations that would jeopardize these feelings.

A second type of stress situation involves those demands which are neither foreseeable nor avoidable. These are *Type B* stress situations. Accidents are of this type, as when a youngster is hit by a baseball while watching a game, or when a teenager who happens to be at a place in school where a fight breaks out gets hurt even though he was not involved. The sudden, unexpected death of a loved one is another example of a stress that is both unforeseeable and unavoidable. Divorce of parents is unthinkable for many teenagers and therefore also unforeseeable and unavoidable.

Type B stress situations usually make the greatest demands upon young people. As we saw in the discussion of divorce, with this type of stress teenagers have to deal with the attitudes of their friends and teachers at the same time that they are struggling with their own feelings. Such stress situations put demands upon young people both from within and from without. A youngster who has been handicapped by an accident,

166

like the teenager who has to deal with divorce, has to adjust to new ways of relating to others as well as new ways of thinking about himself or herself.

Again, the young person with a strong sense of identity and a feeling of self-esteem has the best chance of managing these stress situations as well as they can be managed. In the case of divorce, for example, the teenager who incorporates other people's perspectives with his or her own is able to deal with the situation better than other teenagers who lack this perspective. For example, one young man, who went on to win honors at an Ivy League school, told his father when he and the mother divorced, "You are entitled to live your own life and to find happiness too."

This integrated perspective also helps young people deal with the death of a loved one. If it was an elderly grandparent who had been suffering great pain, the young person can see that from the perspective of the grandparent dying may have been preferable to living a life of agony with no hope of recovery. As one teenager told me with regard to his grandfather who had just died, "He was in such pain, he was so doped up he couldn't really recognize me. I loved him so much I just couldn't stand to see him that way." By enabling the young person to see death from the perspective of others, including that of the person who is dying, the young person is able to mourn the loss but also to get on with life.

The third type of stress situation is one in which the potential stress is foreseeable but not avoidable. This is a *Type* C stress situation. A teenager who has stayed out later than he or she was supposed to foresees an unavoidable storm at home. Likewise, exams are foreseeable but unavoidable stress situations. Being required to spend time with relatives one does not like is another stress situation that the teenager can foresee but not avoid. These are but a few examples of situations the teenager might wish to avoid but must learn to accept as inevitable.

To young people who have attained a solid sense of self and identity, foreseeable and unavoidable stress situations are manageable, again, because of self-esteem and the integrated perspective. They look at the situation from the perspective of themselves as well as that of the other people involved and try to prepare accordingly. They may decide, as one young man of my acquaintance did, that "with my folks, honesty is the best policy. I get into less trouble if I tell the truth than if I make up stories." In the case of visiting relatives they do not like, integrated teenagers see it from the perspective of what it means to others, such as their parents. And with respect to stress situations like exams, because they want to maintain their self-esteem, they prepare for the exam so that they will make a good showing for themselves as well as for others.

It is important to say, too, that integrated teenagers come in any and all personality types. Some are introverted and shy, others are extroverted and fun-loving. Some are preoccupied with intellectual concerns, others primarily with matters of the heart. Despite this diversity, they all share the prime characteristics of the integrated teenager: a set of attitudes, values, and habits that enable the young person to serve self and society, and a strong sense of self-esteem.

To be sure, life is complex and varied. Even the most integrated teenager, of whatever personality type, may occasionally be so overwhelmed by stress that he or she loses the integrated perspective and suffers bouts of low self-esteem. We need to remember that teenagers are new at the game of stress management and have just acquired the skills they need for this purpose. Nonetheless, the general principle holds true. The more integrated the teenager is with respect to self and identity, the better prepared he or she is to manage the basic stress situations.

Stress and Patchwork-Self Personality Types

A patchwork self is the end result of growth by substitution. A teenager with a patchwork self has acquired a set of attitudes, values, and habits that are more or less unconnected with one another. Often these values, attitudes, and habits are in conflict. Indeed, teenagers with a patchwork self often behave as if they always had to choose between giving in to others and looking out for themselves. In addition, they have low self-esteem because they feel bad about themselves if they give in to others but also if they stand up to them.

The teenager with a patchwork self mismanages stress because he or she brings inner conflicts to the basic stress situations, thus making the energy demands so overwhelming that the teenager seeks merely to escape. Teenagers with a patchwork self, like integrated teenagers, come in many different personality types. Some of these patchwork-self personality types are more likely to succumb to one type of stress situation than to another. Accordingly, in our discussion of how patchwork-self teenagers mismanage stress, we will also look at the types most susceptible to particular stress situations.

Type A stress situations often reveal two different types of patchwork-self teenagers, the *anxious teenager* and the *conforming teenager*. Some teenagers, when confronted with foreseeable but avoidable dangers, proceed to worry and stew over their decisions. Because they lack an integrated perspective and a strong sense of self-esteem, they cannot decide whether to avoid the situation or to give in. Many arrive at an alternative solution: they get sick. Anxious teenagers often develop bodily complaints when they are confronted with Type A stress situations.

Dr. Merilee Oaks observes that headaches are particularly common among a group of teenage girls she is encountering in Los Angeles. "I'm seeing a group of teenage girls of Latin origin and they have a lot of psychosomatic symptoms in connection with anger and depression," she says. "These girls are caught in a culture conflict. They are growing up in the freedom of the American culture while living in families with repressive Old World parents and grandparents. These girls don't know how to fight back or express themselves because their cultural mores say that you must not argue with elders. So they have a lot of headaches. I've seen even daily migraine headaches among these girls."[2]

Other anxious teenagers confronted with foreseeable but avoidable dangers develop boredom or fatigue. "I've had a number of teenagers come in to see me complaining of fatigue and excessive sleeping," says Dr. Charles Wibbelsman, a specialist in adolescent medicine. "They often come in saying, 'I think I have mono' or 'I must be anemic or something.' That could be. But often the teenager doesn't have any underlying medical problem. Yet he or she is tired all of the time and sleeps twelve or fourteen hours a day. When a physical disease is not present, this fatigue could well be a sign of anxiety and depression."[3]

Still other anxious teenagers experience stomach pains and disorders. "The gastrointestinal tract, most notably the stomach and intestines, is quite easily affected by the emotions," says Dr. Wibblesman. "It may take a stomach-ache, diarrhea or more alarming symptoms to point out to parents just how tense, depressed, frightened or angry the teenager is feeling."[4]

In all these cases, we can see the underlying characteristics of the patchwork self. Anxious teenagers have low self-esteem and an unconnected and often conflicting set of values, attitudes, and habits. Confronted with foreseeable but avoidable stress situations, they avoid the situation in a self-punishing way. Often these patterns of response to stress are learned in childhood and are called on automatically by teenagers who have not acquired a healthy sense of self and identity.

The conforming teenagers with a patchwork self reveal themselves differently in response to Type A stress situations. In general they have low self-esteem and have not acquired a healthy set of attitudes and habits that would enable them to feel better about themselves. Instead, they often look for a "quick fix" from peer-group approval and acceptance:

> I would never have taken acid if it wasn't offered or if the kid hadn't said "It's such a good time." If the kid said "We don't know what's in this and it might be dangerous, it would mess up your hormones," I don't think I would have taken it. When I took the Quaaludes, everyone else was taking them, so I did it too. It was the same thing with cigarettes. I started because everybody else was smoking them. It wasn't just one or two people. It was everybody I know. I'd go to a party and the whole place would be an ashtray.[5]

Other conforming teenagers give in to the peer pressure to become sexually active:

> I felt sure I was the only virgin left in my crowd and it got to the point where I just wanted to get it over with and be able to say, like everyone else—that I had done it. Otherwise, it was like I was an outsider or a baby or something. I'm not sure it was worth it. I wasn't exactly thrilled by the experience. I felt guilty and bad about myself plus I was disappointed. I kept asking myself, so what's the big deal? But I did it mostly because everybody was doing it or said they were and I didn't want to be out of it.[6]

It is important to remember at this point that peer pressure has no power in and of itself. The peer group is powerful only because there are teenagers with a patchwork self, particularly of the conforming variety, who lack the inner strengths that would weigh against conforming. Anxious teenagers avoid conforming by resorting to bodily complaints and hence to a more childish orientation so that they will not be called upon for serious decision making. Conforming teenagers want to grow up but don't really know how to go about it, so they go along with the crowd. But for both types of teenagers the reaction only furthers growth by substitution and a continued patchwork sense of self.

Teenagers with a patchwork self also have a different perception of Type B stress situations, those that are both unforeseeable and unavoidable. As noted earlier, such situations include accidents, divorce, and death. This type of situation also includes events such as breaking up with a girlfriend or boyfriend, getting raped, or being beaten or robbed. Clearly such stress situations are difficult for the most mature and integrated adult, much less a teenager, to handle. Such events violate our deepest sense of self-esteem and identity. And for young people in the process of constructing a self-definition or for those who have only acquired a patchwork sense of self, such events can be devastating because they undermine what is already a low sense of self-esteem.

Teenagers who are most susceptible to Type B stress situations tend to be of two different kinds. Both kinds tend to see such situations, *not* as events that could happen to anyone, but rather as events directed at them because of their fate or bad luck. One group of teenagers who fall into this pattern is the self-punishers. These young people tend to feel that they are the only ones who ever experience bad things. It is this lack of perspective that makes them believe there is no way out, that they are helpless, hapless, and hopeless. When young people think about themselves and the world in this way, the stage is set for self-destructive behavior:

> I've tried to commit suicide to get even with my mother. I've done crazy things like take pills, but she never knew about it. She's never home to see me go through these fits and torture myself. So the times I take 25 aspirins and 500 milligram pills, and my ears are ringing she doesn't even know. Why do all that if no one's going to react to it? People don't try to reason with you. I only have one friend, a male, I can rap with about it. He doesn't think it's stupid. I don't need to be told that. I just want someone to understand what I'm feeling and try to relate to me. I don't really want to die; I just want to escape.[7]

Not all self-punishing teenagers go so far as to attempt suicide. Many just feel bad about themselves and accept who and what they are as their fate without any sense that they can change:

> I haven't been too happy with myself. But lately I've kind of got back in the swing of things. I'm not my own best friend. I get into a lot of fights with myself. I can feel it inside me, just disagreeing a lot. I state my opinions and somebody will come up with theirs and change mine completely. I wish I could keep hold of mine for a little bit longer. I'm not very sure of myself.

> I'm too fat and I want to be a little taller. Also I have such a soft heart, and I'm very emotional. I don't look at

172

myself as someone who is outstanding. I'm dull. I guess I'm special to the people around me, but to myself I don't feel special at all. I want to be someone special to myself.[8]

Although many self-punishing teenagers talk and behave as if they are demanding love and attention and as if this would solve the problem, the answer is not so simple. At a deeper level many teenagers of this type feel that they are basically unlovable. Indeed, they are often attracted to people who treat them badly because this confirms their deep-down image of themselves. And they distrust those who profess to like and admire them, because they believe such people are being dishonest. Here we see another side of the self-punishing teenager. Such young people perceive what is good for them as bad and what is bad for them as good.

The second type of patchwork-self teenager revealed by situations that are unforeseeable and unavoidable is the competitive one. Such teenagers see Type B situations as a challenge. They believe that they can change their luck. Many young people of this type often become addicted to gambling. They become convinced of the gambler's fallacy, that the more you lose, the more likely you are to win the next time. Unfortunately, the laws of probability don't work that way.

Other competitive teenagers seem to identify themselves with their goals. Getting good grades means being a good person. Such students compete ardently. And even after the tests are scored and graded, they still come in to argue about and fight for points. One student told me, "My father will kill me if I get a C in this course." In some schools the competition is so fierce that students tear out articles of journals left on reserve in the library so that they will have an advantage over their peers. Such young people will not accept the principle of a free market and wish to tilt the forces of chance in their favor. Cheating is another way the competitive teenager tries to beat the odds.

Both the self-punishing and the competitive teenager show the two characteristics that mark the patchwork self: low self-esteem and unconnected attitudes, values, and habits. And again we find the familiar duality of this type of self. They feel that they can advance themselves only by defeating others and that others can advance only by defeating them. Self and society are in constant conflict, and there is little energy to build those aspects of self that will allow the young person to coordinate the interests of self and others and acquire positive self-esteem.

Type C stress situations reveal still other patchwork-self personality types. Stress situations of this variety are foreseeable but not avoidable. Such events include dentist's appointments, visiting relatives whom one violently dislikes, school assignments, and tests. Many troubled families present stress situations of this sort as well. A teenager whose parent drinks and is abusive has a chronic foreseeable but unavoidable stress waiting for him or her at home.

One patchwork-self personality type revealed by Type C situations is the *angry* teenager. What integrated teenagers and adults see as unavoidable demands, angry teenagers see as avoidable impositions, attempts by adults to exercise authority. For angry teenagers, every foreseeable and unavoidable stress situation becomes a battlefield over power and control. Whether it is doing chores, keeping their room clean, or doing homework, nothing is done without a struggle. And, more often than not, nothing gets done.

With the angry teenager, low self-esteem is denied or explained away. Such young people always have an excuse for not doing what they are supposed to be doing. Other people, events, or situations always take the blame; the teenager is never responsible. And such teenagers take umbrage if they are taken to task for not doing their share of chores or their homework. Their attitude often seems to be: "What right have you to ask me to do such menial tasks? After all, I was meant for better things." Not surprisingly, these angry teenagers have the capacity to provoke a lot of anger in their parents and other adults.

In such teenagers, the basic components of the patchwork self are clearly in evidence. There is the low self-esteem, which is projected onto the outside world while the teenager poses as a "cool cat." There are the conflicting and unintegrated attitudes, values, and habits with respect to self and others. By refusing to do what is unavoidable, the young person makes it impossible to find ways of serving both self and society and of getting on with life. Rather, such young people seem "stuck," mired in confrontations that go nowhere and accomplish nothing.

Another variety of patchwork self revealed by Type C stress situations is the *frightened* teenager. These young people perceive foreseeable and unavoidable demands as threatening. With respect to school, for example, whereas the angry teenager is truant, the frightened teenager may display school phobia. As one parent said of her daughter's fear:

> It just got worse and worse. She was so afraid of this nun who yelled at students if they gave the wrong answers or asked questions. She didn't dare ask questions. Her fear got in the way of her understanding the class material and she wasn't doing well. She was so afraid of being yelled at for making a mistake, she avoided going to school whenever possible. Which meant that she got farther and farther behind.[9]

In other teenagers the fear of school masks the fear of separating from the parents. Some teenagers believe, for example, that if their parents are left alone, they will fight and decide to get a divorce.

We see a different variety of frightened teenager in families where a parent is alcoholic, abusive, rejecting, or some combination of these. Such teenagers become increasingly frightened and may eventually run away. But often they go from the "frying pan into the fire" because the world outside is often even more frightening than the home. Many of these young people, however, really have no choice, and many are simply abandoned. We will talk more about runaways in the next chapter.

Frightened teenagers show the by-now familiar components of the patchwork-self personality. They have low self-esteem but believe that their salvation lies in others. They will do almost anything if others will only be nice to them. Yet, by being too accommodating, they invite exploitation and manipulation. Unlike angry teenagers, who always blame others, frightened teenagers always blame themselves. Their efforts at currying favor win neither the respect of others nor self-respect. Again, a disguised case from my files of a frightened *and* self-punishing teenager.

> J. is an extremely overweight fourteen-year-old boy. He is of above-average intelligence and does reasonably well in school. He was brought to see me because he was caught drinking. Apparently he had been buying friends for a number of years. He was currently going with a group of boys who accepted him only because he gave them money and food, most of which he got from home. The boys humiliated him, had him kneel down and kiss their feet, and called him vile names. One day they coerced him into stealing some liquor from his father's bar. The boys got drunk and were found out. It was then that the whole story came out.

In this teenager, as in most young people, there was, nonetheless, a core of integrity and self-respect that he had suppressed out of fear. Once he could deal with his anger at himself, and at his peers, he began to lose weight and to assert himself as he acquired a more cohesive set of attitudes and values about himself and about others. In frightened, self-punishing teenagers, as in the other varieties of the patchwork self, there is still a strong potential for growth. Beneath the conflicting and unconnected ideas, values, and habits is a healthy core waiting to find the means to integrate and serve effectively the demands of self and of society. That inner core of self-esteem and integrity is their hope and ours of an eventually integrated sense of self and identity.

But without help, all too many teenagers with whatever variety of patchwork self will get worse before they get better, if they ever do. And that is the real tragedy of teenagers with a patchwork self. Not only are they unable to avoid, cope with, or prepare for stress (so as to minimize it and manage it), but they also expose themselves to much more stress than they actually need to encounter. As a consequence, they have to spend more and more clock and calendar energy in stress-related activities, leaving less for healthy growth by differentiation. A vicious circle is set in motion whereby the very actions meant to resolve the stress situation merely exacerbate it, which produces more stress reactions with ever more debilitating results.

The vulnerability of the teenager with a patchwork self is made even more serious by the many new or at least more powerful stresses confronting young people in today's society. Even well-integrated young people can be pressured into problem behavior in today's world. Indeed, it is the combination of increased vulnerability and increased stress that accounts for the alarming increase in stress reactions we will deal with next.

Chapter 9

Teenage Reactions to Stress

*T*eenagers today are under more psychological stress than ever before. To make matters worse, a large proportion of today's teenagers have one or another variety of patchwork self, which renders them vulnerable to stress. This lethal combination of increased stress and increased numbers of teenagers who are vulnerable to stress has produced the alarming increase in destructive stress reactions that characterizes the contemporary generation of teenagers.

Psychological Stress

It is not surprising that the same social forces that contribute to the teenager's vulnerability to stress also impose new demands for adjustment. Vanishing markers, to illustrate, not only deprive teenagers of important opportunities for growth by integration, but also present them with new Type A stress situations. That is to say, vanishing markers present young people with many new foreseeable and avoidable stress situations.

Young people today, for example, are freer than ever before to engage in sexual activity, to abuse drugs, and to flout adult authority. At the same time, they are less prepared than ever before to manage these new freedoms. One way in which teenagers, already overburdened with stress or vulnerable thanks to a patchwork self, react to these new freedoms is amusingly illustrated in this anecdote from social psychologist Daniel Yankelovitch:

> A psychologist friend told me an anecdote which had amused and bemused her. A patient in psychotherapy with her, a woman in her mid-twenties, complained that she had become nervous and fretful because life had grown so hectic— too many big weekends, too many discos, too many late hours, too much talk, too much wine, too much pot, too much love making.
>
> "Why don't you stop?" asked the therapist mildly. Her patient stared back blankly for a moment, and then her face lit up, dazzled by an illumination. "You mean I really don't have to do what I want to do?" she burst out in amazement.[1]

This example nicely illustrates how conforming teenagers perceive stress situations that are both foreseeable and avoidable: they see them as *un*avoidable. The example also reflects a compensatory defense process employed by conforming teenagers: the rationalization that when they give in to peer pressure they are doing what they want to do.

Another powerful Type A stress confronting today's teenagers is the threat of environmental degradation and of nuclear war. Both are foreseeable and avoidable, but they are not under the teenager's control. They are anxiety-provoking, particularly to anxious teenagers who are sensitive to this type of stress. Listen to the statements of teenagers who have just seen a film depicting some of the horrors of Hiroshima:

> *Alex:* Well some people didn't have much choice, but if I saw my parents and the rest of the community lying down— twisted—I think that I would commit suicide.
>
> I'm scared that a war is going to start. I'm scared that it could happen at any time, you know 1, 2, 3 boom! And that would be it.
>
> *Jack:* I learned that it is not as if the bomb struck and everybody laid down and died. Everybody is torn in all directions at once

and it is burning, and you don't recover from something like that.

I don't know what I think. I don't know what I'm supposed to think. I'm against it.

I care that somebody is going to get crazy and start pushing the button. Then they're going to blow up Russia and they are going to blow us up. We're going to die and they are going to die, and everything is going to be as primitive as it was a billion years ago.[2]

This type of stress is difficult enough for adults to manage. We should not be surprised that it is at least equally difficult for teenagers.

Family permutations, so common in contemporary American society, also impose powerful stresses upon teenagers in addition to rendering them more vulnerable to stress. Family permutations confront teenagers with a Type B stress situation, namely, one in which the stress is both unforeseeable and unavoidable. Such stresses can include not only the divorce of parents but also the separation from friends as a consequence of a move necessitated by divorce.

Fourteen-year-old Melanie, for example, lost interest in hobbies and school and started sleeping a lot after her family moved from New Jersey to the San Francisco Bay area. Her mother, worried that something might be physically wrong with Melanie, took her to see Dr. Charles Wibbelsman of the Northern Permanente Medical Group, who says:

> There was nothing physically wrong with Melanie, but in talking to her I discovered that the family move had separated her from her best friend—a very significant person in her life—and she was greatly affected by this. Adults may tend to minimize such a loss. After all, we have more experience in coping with such separation. We know we can keep in touch, meet new friends and take care of ourselves. But these facts are not obvious to the teenager. A close friend is a salient part of his or her life. Also such partings are usually the result of parental choice or transfer. When someone else makes the decision to move, the teenager suffers not only

the loss of a friend, but also the sense of lacking control over his or her destiny. Some kids whose parents move frequently have problems with peer relationships—and are subject to periodic or chronic depression.[3]

The stress of loss, then, can come in many different forms and from many different directions. It is a form of stress that almost every teenager today has to cope with. If the teenager happens to have a patchwork self of the type most vulnerable to this form of stress—namely, if he or she is self-punishing or competitive—the teenager may engage in destructive escape behaviors.

The contemporary American high school is another institution in today's society that not only renders teenagers more vulnerable to stress but also presents them with "awesome" Type C stress situations. High schools, as they are run today, present teenagers with a seemingly endless series of foreseeable and unavoidable demands. Consider the following announcement made over a public address system by an assistant high school principal which appears in Ernest Boyer's book, *Highschool*:

> May I have your attention. Anyone who was not on time this morning must report to the principal's office with a late slip within the next half hour. If late slips are not turned in by then you will be marked absent for the day. Also, anyone who was not here yesterday must turn in an absence slip. If you were late yesterday and do not have an excused absence, please see me immediately.
>
> Next, I have to report more incidents of smoking in the third floor men's room. That room, as a result, will be closed, and students will use the men's room on either the first or second floor. In case some of you have forgotten, let me repeat: students caught smoking anywhere in the building will face dismissal from school according to school regulations.
>
> My next announcement is a disgrace to this school and to its student body. The north side of the building has for the fifth time this year been smeared with graffiti. Until the stu-

dent who defaced the building comes forth and owns up, I'm taking the precaution of confining all students to the interior of the building during the day until further notice.

Finally, I have to remind you again that you are not to linger in the halls between classes. At the sound of the bell, go promptly to your class. Anyone caught in the halls after the last bell without a pass report to me.[4]

For those teenagers already vulnerable to Type C stress, namely, those with a patchwork self who are angry or frightened, such announcements may trigger defensive reactions. Even teenagers who are not especially vulnerable to this type of stress are hassled by some of the foreseeable but unavoidable stresses of the contemporary high school. The lawlessness of schools, the prevalence of theft, sexual activity, violence, and substance abuse, is difficult to prepare for even if you can foresee it. A sixteen-year-old boy describes it this way:

School is not my favorite thing but at least you get a chance to be with your friends. There are plenty of hassles though, because some of the kids are totally obnoxious. I've had lunch money stolen from me when I was younger, and I was picked on plenty even last year. But this year it's better. Last year one of the kids who's about six feet tall (I'm short) picked me up and held me over an open stair well, two stories up. I was sure he was going to drop me down. But I stayed pretty cool and I guess I wasn't interesting enough for him since I didn't scream or anything, so he let me go. Later on I used to give him quarters so he became my protector of sorts. If any of the other kids would go after me, he'd come to my rescue. It worked pretty well until he got kicked out of school. You really have to learn how to survive.[5]

Schools, then, like vanishing markers and family permutations, stress today's teenagers as never before. At the same time, of course, they render teenagers more vulnerable to stress by encouraging growth by substitution and a patchwork sense of self. But even teenagers who have attained an integrated sense of self and identity can be made vulnerable if many dif-

183

ferent demands for adjustment are made upon them at the same time. And the possibility of being overwhelmed by stress is much more imminent today, when the likelihood of stress at home, at school, and in the larger society is much greater than in the past.

When stress becomes too great, more than the teenager can manage (either because there is too much at once or because the teenager mismanages it), the teenager's major aim becomes escape. Unfortunately, escape devices are only temporary solutions and do not get at the real problems. They are also destructive and many times will do permanent harm. The particular escape device chosen by a teenager will depend upon his or her personality and life situation. Nonetheless, certain types of stress do tend to provoke particular types of escape devices. The prevalence of these escape devices among today's teenagers speaks both to their vulnerability and to the powerful demands for adjustment society makes upon them.

Reactions to the Stress of Freedom

Freedom (a Type A stress) puts teenagers under tremendous stress indirectly, in that they are subject to peer pressure to exercise freedom. This pressure gives rise to a great deal of anxiety, which is often reduced only by giving in to the pressure. Anxious teenagers who refuse to give in or who are under stress from other directions as well may develop physical symptoms of stress such as headaches and stomachaches. In a recent study, physicians reported that 30 percent of teenagers appearing at the adolescent clinic for treatment of physical complaints were also suffering from underlying anxiety and depression.

Although we have no reliable statistics on the prevalence of psychosomatic complaints among teenagers, the incidence is likely to be very high. One reason for the inadequacy of statistics is that when teenagers are troubled, it is easier for them to ask for medical than for psychological help. Young people worry that others will think that they are "crazy" if they go to see a psychiatrist or psychologist. It is however, wrong to dismiss a teenager's headaches and stomachaches as "phony," even if they are caused by anxiety. "I cringe when I hear someone say, 'It's just a psychosomatic pain,' says Dr. Marilyn Mehr, a specialist in adolescent medicine. "The implication is that if it's psychosomatic, it isn't real. But of course the pain we see is real, both emotionally and physically."[6]

Other teenagers, often of the conforming type, give in to the peer pressure. The extent of teenage drinking gives some idea of the number of vulnerable teenagers as well as the stresses all teenagers are experiencing today. The National Institute on Alcohol Abuse and Alcoholism reports, conservatively, that 1.3 million Americans between the ages of twelve and seventeen have serious drinking problems. A report from the Department of Health, Education and Welfare recently stated that more than 3 million youths nationwide have experienced problems at home, school, or on the highways as a result of drinking.[7] An analysis of more than one hundred surveys conducted on teenage drinking practices in the United States between 1941 and 1975 showed that the proportion of high school students who reported being drunk at least once rose dramatically from 19 percent before 1966 to 49 percent by 1975.[8] And former surgeon general Julius B. Richmond reports that death rates for young adults and adolescents are worse today than twenty years ago—and mixing alcohol and drugs with driving is to blame for much of that toll.[9]

Teenage drinking is not a new phenomenon and certainly occurred in previous generations, but the number of young people who are drinking today is, to the best of our knowledge, greater than ever before. In part this is a reflection of the affluence of our society. Alcoholic beverages are expensive, and only in an affluent society such as ours do young people have enough disposable income to buy it regularly.

Affluence and peer pressure are perhaps the most immediate causes of the alarming amount of teenage drinking, but there are background causes that operate as well. Some of these are the hardest for adults to deal with. As the following observations by some teenagers make clear, a parent's drinking behavior clearly plays a role in determining a teenager's approach to alcohol.

> *Ray:* I'd like to drink like my mother. She knows when to quit and she never drinks too much. She can hold it. That's the way I'd like to drink. I don't always. Usually she drinks at home. When I drink, I like to do it at home. I don't like to go out, it's more comfortable.
>
> *Chris:* My folks are probably the most accomplished social drinkers in town. Every night, promptly at 5:30 the booze comes out and they party. Dancing at the club. Dancing here and there, running all over. I really love their life-style. They get high enough so that everyone's having a good time. Not squashed.[10]

Parental example is important, but it is far from the whole story. Whatever the background the immediate causes for teenage drinking, once the pattern is established it is maintained. Teenagers today drink for the same reason adults do, namely, to relieve stress. They do not drink to imitate adults or to play at being grown up. Rather, because they have had adulthood thrust upon them, they look upon drinking as a right and prerogative of their adult estate.

There is a similar pattern for substance abuse. According to the results of several studies, substance abuse has grown alarmingly in recent years. A study compiled for the Department of Health, Education and Welfare in 1978 revealed that one in nine high school seniors was smoking marijuana daily—almost double the number of users in 1975.[11] Other studies reveal the extent to which our entire population is becoming a drug culture:

> In 1962 less than 4 percent of the population had ever used an illegal drug. Two decades later, according to the National Institute on Drug Abuse, 33 percent of Americans age 12 and older reported having used marijuana, hallucinogens, cocaine, heroin, or psychotherapeutic drugs for nonmedical purposes at some time.
>
> Sixty-four percent of American young people have tried

186

an illegal drug before they finish high school, and more than a third have used drugs other than marijuana, according to another 1982 National Institute study. The research showed that 59 percent of the high school seniors had tried marijuana, 16 percent had tried LSD and 1 percent had tried heroin.[12]

There are many reasons why teenagers use drugs, but the most immediate in most cases is peer pressure. Substance abuse, from the perspective of an integrated personality, is a foreseeable and avoidable danger. Although many youngsters with such a personality may try drugs once, much as they might try a roller coaster once, drug use remains an avoidable danger. But when the young person is hit with stress from many sides, or if he or she has primarily a conforming patchwork self, the peer group pressure is perceived differently. To such young people, going along with the peer group is a foreseeable but unavoidable risk situation. And the compensatory rationalization is "I am grown up and I have the right to do as I please."

The Stress of Loss

Regardless of its source, the experience of loss (a Type B stress) gives rise to depression. We have already considered many of the possible sources of this depression—death, divorce, environmental degradation, and the threat of nuclear war. How young people handle depression depends upon both the kind of self they have constructed and the amount of stress they have to deal with.

For teenagers who are self-punishers, the stress of loss often leads to one of several destructive escape devices. For example, sexual "acting out" (of unconscious anger against the parents) is frequently observed in teenage girls who have lost their fathers through divorce. This pattern emerges in adolescence even though the loss itself may have occurred in childhood. This happens because children do not really understand divorce, and it is only when they reach adolescence and begin thinking in a new key that its significance hits them with full force. Such young women often become very seductive and bold with men, particularly older men. Here is the response of a teenager girl to the question "How do you think not having a father in your house for most of your life affected you?"

> I know me, and I can see it in my sister too. I'm always looking for some guy I can confide in. Maybe a teacher. Not so much a teacher, but like this couple I worked for this summer. I'm really close with them. They're young and the guy couldn't be my father because he's too young, but I can confide in him . . . .
>
> My older sister . . . was pretty wild when she was in high school. Really into drugs. I don't know if the divorce had anything to do with it. She'd go out and get wasted, and started skipping school a lot.
>
> My little sister falls in love with her teachers. She finds reasons to stay in school a lot. If I were her, if I really wanted to see my father, I'd get mad and call him up. But I don't think she ever does.[13]

Confronted with the stress of loss, some self-punishing teenagers may attempt suicide. Suicide is currently the third leading cause of death among young people after substance abuse and accidents. In 1977 almost five thousand young people between the ages of fifteen and twenty-four committed suicide. This was an increase of 131 percent from 1961 to 1975. Over the past two and a half decades, suicides have increased dramatically for younger age groups. For ten-to-fourteen-year-olds the increase has been 166 percent; for fifteen-to-nineteen-year-olds, 192 percent, and for the twenty-to-twenty-four-year olds, 194 percent.[14]

Many different theories of suicide have been offered, but all suggest that there is a background of depression that, together with a contemporary experience, can trigger the suicidal act. Such losses include:

1. The death of a family member
2. The divorce or separation of parents

3. Personal or family problems with the law
4. Personal injury or chronic illness of the adolescent or a close family member or friend
5. The marriage of a sibling or the remarriage of a parent
6. Being fired from a job or a parent's being fired from a job
7. The retirement of a parent
8. A drastic change in the health of a close family member or friend
9. The adolescent's own pregnancy, abortion, or birth of a baby or that of a sibling or parent[15]

Some of these nine experiences are far more common today than they were only a few years ago. And they are testimony to the increase in stress confronting today's teenager. For most adults with a healthy sense of reality, most of the experiences listed here would not destroy their grasp of reality. But for a teenager, particularly a self-punishing one, these experiences can be devastating. The following report by a teenager who attempted suicide illustrates how the combination of overwhelming stress and the feeling, common to self-punishers, that misfortune was her lot contributed to her suicidal act:

> Last summer, I tried to kill myself. I was 15 and I couldn't seem to cope with life anymore.
> I swallowed a handful of Tetracycline and 15 little pink pills—hydro something. Since the name was so hard to pronounce, I figured they had to be dangerous.
> Everything was wrong, I didn't have anyone to talk to. I don't know exactly what I was, I just wasn't feeling right about myself. I felt inadequate, like I wasn't worth anything. I thought nobody loved or needed me, my relationship with my mother, which had been deteriorating since she divorced my dad, was getting worse. On top of that, my boyfriend— the first boyfriend I ever made love with, had just broken up with me.
> As soon as I told my girlfriend about the pills, she came over to drive me to the hospital. The doctor made me throw

189

up. Then he sent me to a family therapist. Mom goes with me every week and I guess we are finally starting to understand each other.[16]

There are many different dynamics and patterns to suicide, but often the immediate and precipitating causes are stress coming from many sides at once and the feeling, indeed the conviction, that one is not worthy or is fated to bad luck and misfortune. It cannot be emphasized enough that any mention or allusion to suicide on the part of a teenager *must* be taken seriously. If that happens, the best thing to do is to contact a professional for guidance and counsel.

Another pattern of response by self-punishing teenagers to the experience of loss is self-starvation, or anorexia nervosa. This severe eating disorder is afflicting an increasing number of teenage girls (about 95 percent of anorexia victims are girls).[17] It is estimated that about 280,000 young women aged twelve to twenty-five suffer from anorexia in the United States. The prevalence of this illness and its potential lethal consequences were highlighted by the death of pop singer Karen Carpenter in February 1983. Apparently this successful young performer succumbed to heart failure as a consequence of her extreme, self-induced weight loss.[18]

Most anorexics come from middle to upper-middle-class homes and have a history of being "good," "well-behaved" young people who were model daughters and students. At a deeper level anorexics feel very ineffective as individuals and believe that they have little if any control over their lives. Dr. Regina Casper says, "One can recognize a paralyzing sense of ineffectiveness which pervades all of their thinking and actions. People suffering from eating disorders experience themselves as acting only in response to demands coming from others and as not doing anything because they want to."[19]

Anorexia is often initiated by a particular incident. Such incidents are of the kind that, for most people, might prompt little more than a slight annoyance at the way we gain weight.

But for the anorexic or potential anorexic, the experience can be critical:

> Judy, a fifteen-year-old anorectic, was shopping with her mother for a new pair of jeans when her mother remarked that Judy's stomach was really beginning to stick out unattractively. Her mother went on to say that whenever her daughter put on a few pounds, it seemed to go to the same spot. She suggested that they purchase one or two overblouses for Judy.
>
> In response, Judy sucked in her stomach and took a long hard look at herself in the mirror. At that moment her stomach appeared enormous to her. She decided that she didn't like the jeans she had on or any of the other pairs she tried on subsequently. Judy left the store without making any purchases. That evening she began a strict diet that eventually turned into anorexia nervosa.[20]

Anorexics, then, are depressed over what they don't have (a good figure, control over themselves and others) rather than over what they have had and lost. Their dieting is an attempt to gain control over themselves and others (they manipulate parents with their poor health and appearance). But this solution to the stress of loss only creates more stress and may even be fatal. Anorexics also provide a good example of how growth by substitution can be deceptive and can give the appearance of greater personality integration than actually exists.

The Stress of Frustration

The third source of stress for the contemporary teenager comes primarily from the school. School presents teenagers with a Type C stress, one that is foreseeable but not avoidable. The other major source of Type C stress is the family. This is particularly true for those teenagers who must come home each day to a house ridden with tension and bickering or to an alcoholic and/or abusive parent.

Teenagers who are most susceptible to the stress of schooling are the angry type of patchwork-self personalities. Although they are stressed in many different ways, school becomes the focal point of their reaction. I should say here that the area in which a teenager chooses to engage in destructive escape behavior is frequently the area that the parents are most sensitive about. Our children know us very well, and they can play on our sensitivities. If we are overly concerned about their health, they may develop psychosomatic symptoms or anorexia. And if we are concerned about schooling, they may become truant or drop out. For teenagers, stress reactions are not only escape devices, they are also a means of paying their parents back for all the sins, real or imagined, that the parents committed when the teenagers were children.

Although there are many different reasons why teenagers do poorly at school, getting back at parents for whom schooling is important is, in many cases, part of the problem. To get some idea of the dynamics of poor school performance we can look at some findings from California, inasmuch as it has a higher school dropout rate than any other state. A recent report from the California Assembly Office of Research revealed that the state's truancy and dropout rate among students twelve to seventeen years old is about three times the national average. Although pregnancy and marriage were cited as significant factors in truancy and school dropouts, reasons most often given by students for truancy included dislike of or boredom with school, family or personal problems, academic problems, and difficulties with social adjustment.

Those experienced with counseling truant teenagers agree that these are all significant factors. "Some kids feel that school has nothing to offer and have friends who are also truant or who have dropped out," says school counselor Sarah Napier. "Some kids are simply overwhelmed by the pressures and expectations and can't cope."[21]

Unfortunately, once an angry teenager begins to project his or her inadequacies onto the school, a chain reaction is often set off because in most cases the young person gets away with it and then proceeds to up the ante. Pretty soon the angry

192

teenager may see any and all parental and social demands as dumb and unnecessary. In the extreme, the angry teenager ends up in the category that the Toughlove program was designed to help.

In their homes these teenagers are:
Living in filthy bedrooms and saying that it is their room and they can do what they want.
Fighting with their siblings and saying that their brothers and sisters started it.
Fighting with their parents and saying that Mom or Dad was nagging them.
Consistently coming home late and saying they forgot the time, ran out of gas, their watch was slow.
Stealing objects from their homes and denying it.
Stealing money from parents, grandparents, brothers and sisters and denying it.
Bringing home rude, unkempt people and blaming the family for making their friends feel uncomfortable.
Playing their stereos at all hours and at ear shattering levels and claiming they were only listening to music.
Coming home drunk or stoned frequently and saying they were just partying.
Breaking doors, walls, and furniture and claiming that their family does not understand them.
Lying around the house all day and staying out all night and saying they cannot find a job.
Concerning school issues they are:
Getting suspended because teachers are hassling them.
Playing hooky because school is boring and they want to get a job.
Fighting with teachers because they accuse them falsely.
Failing because teachers have it in for them, school is boring and they have a learning disability.
Not bringing home their report card because they forgot it, lost it, owe money to the library.
Concerning employment issues they are:
Getting fired because the boss was hassling them.
Quitting jobs because they are boring.
Not having money for bills because they did not get paid, lost the money, owed the money to others.[22]

Unfortunately, as this all-too-common pattern indicates, once an angry teenager sees one foreseeable and avoidable demand as avoidable, he or she soon sees all of them in the same way. In my experience with teenagers who fall into this pattern, one thing stands out. They always have a "story." The story always absolves the teenager from any responsibility for responding to foreseeable and unavoidable demands. It is always the dumb boss or the stupid teacher who is at fault.

Because these problems, like those of drugs and alcoholism, are social problems as well as family problems, they have to be dealt with by groups of parents working together to support one another. The Toughlove program, like those designed to help teenagers who abuse drugs and alcohol, is based upon group dynamics, and rightfully so, for like cures like. Since many teenage problems today have peer pressure as their immediate cause, it makes sense to use peer pressure as well as the assertion of adult authority to help change these patterns.

A very different reaction to foreseeable and avoidable situations comes from teenagers who fall into the frightened category. Confronted with an intolerable school situation, the frightened teenager may develop school phobia, as we have seen. However, a frightened teenager confronted with a tension-ridden home situation may decide to run away. Not surprisingly, as home situations have become more stressful as a consequence of divorce, single-parent homes, and blended families, the number of teenage runaways has increased as well.

Although it is difficult to get accurate statistics on the number of teenagers who run away each year (because so many are not reported), the figures we do have are troubling enough. It is estimated that some 600,000 teenagers were runaways in 1970, and more than a million in 1980. This last figure is even more significant when we realize that the absolute number of teenagers was smaller in 1980 than in 1970.

The reasons today's teenagers give for running away from home are different from those given by teenage runaways of a decade ago. "In the 1960's," says Cynthia Myers of the National Runaway Switchboard, "it was more common for kids to run to something. They ran to an environment, a lifestyle or to find

194

something. Now they are running away from something."[23] "Early on we had a lot of traditional runaway situations," notes Roy Jones, the director of the Detroit Transit Alternative. "There was a conflict in the home about going to college or staying up late or the young person was really out just to get a new experience. Now it is much more a survival issue."[24] And Judy Bucy, director of the National Network of Runaway and Youth Services, says, "Ten years ago, if parents could not cope they'd just place the children somewhere until they could cope. Now they decide they don't want the kids around anymore."[25]

What young people are running away from today are such parental actions as physical abuse, incest, and neglect. One runaway girl, Tiffany, is fifteen years old, "a tall delicate 10th grader who wants to be a hairdresser and who likes to wear eyeshadow. In the quiet of a large green house, a few blocks from the State Capitol, she described the last time she saw her father, a few Fridays ago, when he dragged her by the hair into the kitchen and slammed her head against the refrigerator door."[26] Tiffany has found refuge in a shelter for teenagers set up as the result of legislation passed in 1973 called the Runaway Youth Act. (This legislation was passed in response to the discovery in Houston of the mutilated bodies of some twenty boys, all presumed to have been runaways.)

Like so many escape devices, running away only adds to the stresses that teenagers will experience. "Arriving in a strange city with no money, no job, and no skills, the young person is often unaware of the help that is available from runaway shelters across the country. And most teenagers are easy prey out on the streets. There are people who are good at spotting confused kids like that in urban areas," says Veronica Reed of San Francisco's Huckleberry House. "They come up and tell them they know how they can make some money.[27]

Many runaways become prostitutes because it is the only way they can make money and survive. The case of Cathy is typical.

Cathy grew up in a suburb of Seattle reared by her aunt and uncle. Two years ago they moved and left her.

"I went downtown," Cathy said; "I had no place to go. I stayed in hotels around and, if I didn't have any money, I stayed up all night. My mom left me and never did come back. It hurts me how I've been living and how people been treating me." She spoke barely above a whisper. "I get lonely, I keep thinking about my past. I could a had fun, but my mom didn't care for me. What kind of mom is that? I see all these other kids with their moms that get lots of love. On the street, the kids help one another and take care of one another. Though we don't have money. In a way I love em. I try to treat little kids like my mom should a treated me."

"I started turning tricks when I was thirteen. I never had sex till then. He was nice, about 50 I guess. I didn't have to do anything bad. I didn't know nothing about sex. Everytime I was with a trick I was scared. I felt bad, always being with someone I didn't know, because you don't ever know if you'll end up dead or beat up or something. I tried to get jobs. I had applications but I always was too young or something. There ain't much younger girls can do."

"Have you stopped tricking?"

"Yes," Cathy whispered, "when I lost my baby."[28]

Dotsin Rader, who has studied runaways by talking with them on the streets, has this to say about the fate of many of these young people:

> Runaways in the streets for more than a month usually end up as prostitutes because they have no other way to make do. They will remain in it, on the average, for at least three years . . . .
>
> There are local and national call services and "buy-a-kid" rings from which customers can purchase a runaway child for a night or permanently. In New York, runaways told me the cost of buying a child for life was $5,000.00 It's cheaper elsewhere. In San Diego, I interviewed a runaway who had been sold by his grandfather for $500.
>
> Many runaway children don't live long—150,000 disappear each year. They also suffer from malnutrition, drug related disorders, sexual dysfunction and, having little access to medical care (runaways don't have health insurance), from

disease of all types. A major cause of death among boys engaged in prostitution is rectal hemorrhage.[29]

The plight of runaways tears at our hearts and sympathies, just as the stories told us by the truants from school and life arouse our anger. We cannot paint all teenagers with the same brush. Some deserve our understanding, others our anger, still others our compassion. They all need our help. And because the problems are social problems, produced by society at large and not by parents alone, the help has to be social as well. The Appendix lists programs and services for teenagers engaged in self-destructive stress escape mechanisms.

The best cure of all, of course, is prevention.

Chapter 10

Helping Teenagers Cope

*T*he epidemic of teenage problem behavior in America today is serious and frightening. When 50 percent of the youth in this country have used alcohol and drugs to excess, we have a serious social problem that is getting out of hand. Our first task as parents, educators, and health professionals is to admit that the problem exists and that it will not go away but will only get worse unless we take concerted action. Fortunately, this is already happening in many parts of the country as a growing number of programs such as Toughlove, Parents Anonymous, Parental Stress Lines, and the National Runaway Switchboard provide help and support for troubled teenagers and their parents.

However welcome and needed these programs are, they are still remedial and can do nothing to stem the tide of troubled teenagers. What can we do to prevent some of the human waste and misery that is so endemic to young people today?

Before looking at what we can do, it is important to acknowledge what we cannot do. We cannot, for example, turn the clock back to an earlier, less complex, and less terrifying time. We cannot change the pace of technological change, defuse the knowledge explosion, or fight the computer revolution. Likewise, the threats of nuclear war, environmental degradation, pollution, and cancer-causing chemicals in the food chain will remain a menace that we have to contend with. Although these are foreseeable and avoidable dangers, it will take the highest qualities of our humanness to avoid the unthinkable.

Although these stresses contribute to the problems of teenagers, we have to accept them pretty much as givens. We have, however, much more control over events in the home, at school, and in the media. It is in these domains that we have to look for ways to prevent or at least lessen the amount of teenage destructive stress behavior. We can do this both by helping young people attain a differentiated conception of self and identity and by reducing some of the stresses they encounter.

Encouraging Growth by Integration

What Parents Can Do

As parents, we carry the primary responsibility for the development of our youth and for helping them in their efforts to attain an integrated sense of self and identity. Growth by differentiation and integration takes effort and energy on the part of parents as well as teenagers, but the energy we invest in helping teenagers grow in this manner will pay rich dividends later.

The first and most basic thing we can do as parents to help young people along the path of differentiation is to say no. In saying no, we have to distinguish between what young people want and what they need. A teenage girl who wants to stay out as late as her girlfriends has a want, not a need. If we know that parties begin to deteriorate after midnight, it is reasonable to request that the girl leave parties by twelve.

One father told me the following story: "My wife and I set a firm curfew for our daughter. She didn't like it and gave us a hard time about it. But we stood firm, and despite her complaints she did come home when she was supposed to. One night when she came home from a party, she had a little smile, almost a grin. When I asked her about it she said, 'Oh, Dad, you remember Barbara and Jean who are always teasing me about coming home early. Well, they were bragging about not having to go home when these two creeps came along and started bothering them. I told them I had to go home but they were stuck!'" The frequency with which I hear such stories from teenagers and parents alike is testimony to the strong desire of young people to live in an orderly and caring world.

When I talk to parents about saying no to teenagers, some worry that it will not do any good and that "they do what they want anyway." It is certainly true that it only weakens our authority when we lay down rules that we cannot enforce and that the teenager knows he or she can break with impunity. But we can still say, "I don't want you to smoke because it is bad for your health. I know that you can smoke when you are elsewhere. But each time I find out about it, you will be grounded and have your allowance cut in half." Just because we don't have total control doesn't mean we have no control.

Other parents fail to say no simply to avoid confrontation. If they are hassled at work, are tired or worried about a myriad of things, it is difficult to get into battles about curfews, clothing, friends, and so on. It is easier to give in. But we pay an inordinate price for such giving in. Teenagers will fight limits and rules and may say things to the effect that the parent is a bad person, old-fashioned, unfeeling, et cetera, et cetera. But at a deeper level teenagers know that the parent has risked this recrimination out of caring, and they appreciate it. They just have a very peculiar way of showing that appreciation!

A teenager I talked to in California put the matter quite clearly when she said, "Why does it always have to be my decision? Why can't my dad just say, 'You can't go'? I think that if somebody really loves you, they don't just let you do whatever you want."

Some parents tell me that they cannot say no because the peer-group pressure is too great. There is no denying the power of peer-group and social pressure, particularly when it comes from other parents as well as teenagers. But giving in to pressure is a losing game. *Deal with principle, not with pressure.* If a young teenager wants to have beer at a party, the principle is clear: young teenagers should not have free access to alcohol, period. Likewise, if a mother believes, on principle, that a girl of seven or eight is too young to have her ears pierced and that the youngster should wait until she is old enough to make a reasoned choice on her own, the mother should stick to it regardless of what other mothers and daughters are doing. But only assert principles that you really believe in and are committed to.

In this connection it is wise to remember the words of Ralph Waldo Emerson in his essay "Self-Reliance": "A political victory, a rise of rents, the recovery of a sick friend, or some other external event raises your spirits and you think good days are preparing for you. Do not believe it. It can never be so. Nothing can bring you peace but yourself. Nothing can bring you peace but the triumph of principles."[1] If we give in to pressure, rather than make the matter one of principle, we only set ourselves up for more of the same in the future. Blackmail begets blackmail.

In addition to saying no, we can help our children grow by differentiation and integration by being *persistent*. Many parents say, "I told him not to play his stereo loud, but he just doesn't listen." On inquiry I discover that the father or mother told the youngster a couple of times and then gave up and went elsewhere. As parents, we sometimes need to be as plodding and as repetitious as our offspring. It doesn't pay to be too imaginative or inventive. If there is something we don't like, we should say so simply and directly, over and over again. Messy rooms are a case in point. Often the teenager wears us down by being so persistent in his or her messiness. We have to be equally persistent in our response. If, in response to our request that the room be cleaned up, the teenager complains, "You've told me that a hundred times already," we can say in return, "And *you* have left your room messy more than two hundred times, so you are still ahead of the game." It is not easy for us to be plodding and dogmatic, but it is necessary if the teenager is to learn that he or she cannot wear us down.

A third strategy that we can use to help teenagers acquire an integrated sense of identity is exemplified by the saying *"Strike while the iron is hot."* There is nothing so stale as a warmed-over emotion. When a teenager does something or says something that hurts us or that we don't like, we need to deal with it at the time. To be sure, if it happens in a public place or at a social gathering, we may want to wait till we get the young person alone. But sometimes we may even want to say something publicly so that we don't give others the impression we are willing to accept abuse from our offspring.

Young people have to learn that whereas physical hurts go away in time, those caused by words can last a lifetime. If we don't speak up about our feelings, we only harbor and build up our anger for an uncontrolled explosion later. Moreover, if the issue is not resolved, it continues to preoccupy us and take up some of our much-needed calendar energy. It is much better to get such things out in the open and over with so that we can go on with other things. And we need to remember, too, that there is never going to be a "good" time to deal with these matters. The best time is always the present.

I myself learned this principle the hard way. One of my sons once told me that I mumbled when I talked. Since my business, as a teacher and lecturer, involves a lot of talking, this remark bothered me for a long time, though I didn't say anything about it. I became self-conscious while lecturing, and if I didn't mumble before, I must have begun thereafter. When I finally confronted him with the remark, he said that he was only doing it for my benefit—"constructive criticism," he called it. Psychologist or not, I was sorely tempted to use physical abuse to express my reaction. It would have been much better for me and for my son had I dealt with the remark when it was made.

Still another principle for helping teenagers develop a healthy sense of self and identity is one that, as a psychologist I find awkward to advocate. Since it goes against my psychological training, as a parent I did not use it often enough. In retrospect it was probably my greatest failing as a father. The principle, simply stated, is *Don't understand too much.*

I was trained to try to understand people's behavior and to be nonjudgmental. Although that is a necessary strategy for dealing with patients, it is not a good approach to rearing children. Sometimes bad manners, hurtful remarks, and thoughtless actions are simply that and do not need to be interpreted any further. Maybe that is what Freud had in mind when he reputedly said, "Sometimes a cigar is just a good smoke."

We really do not help teenagers when we try to understand too much. Teenagers need to experience at home the kinds of standards and values they can expect to face in the larger world. When young people are at school or get a job, their teachers and employers are not going to take the trouble to understand their motivations. People will take them at face value. Work is a case in point. Either they get the job done or they don't keep the job. If we understand too much, we fail to prepare our teenagers for the world outside the home.

A last strategy that can help young people acquire a constructive sense of self might be phrased as follows: *Talk, don't communicate.* In my opinion, the term "communication" has been much overused in the literature on parenting. We are told we need to communicate with our offspring, and we are often given various formulas for saying things in the "right" way. Such formulas are probably useful if we remember to use them. But I know that when I am upset, it is hard to remember the specific formula I read about several days earlier.

Rather than learn to follow a specific script when conversing with our teenagers, we need simply to *talk*. The term "communication" suggests that we have a specific message and our only problem is having the time, the opportunity, or the right words to get that message across. But in my experience with teenagers I have found the problem is somewhat different. The true problem is that teenagers are really not quite sure what it is that is bothering them. They need to talk in a rather free-wheeling way in order to discover what they want to say to us. I have a similar experience when I write. Often I am not sure exactly what I want to say until I start writing. Talking, like writing, can help us clarify our thoughts.

We need to allow time for talk with our teenagers without pressuring them to "say what they have to say" and to get on with it. Such talk, which can, initially, center on music, films, friends, or politics, can help young people find out what they are really thinking and feeling. Talking can also help them compare those feelings and thoughts with how others feel and think. The simple matter of talking—open-ended conversation—will let the teenager reflect upon his or her experience. And it is only experience that has been reflected upon that is really of value in the understanding of ourselves and of others.

All of these strategies grow naturally out of a more overriding parental strategy, namely, the exercise of parental authority, a concept that is badly misunderstood in contemporary society. Exerting parental authority doesn't mean that we can't play ball with our children or joke with them or have fun with them. Being a parent doesn't mean being an ogre or a relentless disciplinarian. Rather it means asserting ourselves as adults who have more experience, knowledge, and skill than our offspring. Children and teenagers are young and inexperienced. They very much need and want guidance and instruction from us.

It has to be emphasized that the assertion of adult authority is different from the assertion of adult power. Power is always based on superior force, whereas authority is always based on superior wisdom, knowledge, and skill. A thief with a gun has power, but a skilled teacher, carpenter, or surgeon has authority. As parents we know much more about child rearing than we give ourselves credit for. If we were well parented as children, we have the best training for parenthood that we could possibly obtain. Even if we had a bad childhood, we know a great deal about people and about human relations that we can put to use as parents. The Golden Rule, for example, applies in our relations with children as it does in our relations with other adults.

In my experience in working with parents, in all parts of the country and at all social class levels and with many different ethnic groups, the exercise of authority seems to be the hardest parental task of all. Parents do put pressure on children—to achieve at school, to have friends, to do well in sports, music, dance, and a variety of other extracurricular activities. But this pressure or hurrying of children is not an exercise of parental authority. It is often an abuse of adult power. Hurrying is not based on the parent's superior wisdom, knowledge, and experience; rather it derives from the parent's power to coerce. Most of all, it reflects parent need, not child need.

It is essential that we assert our true authority as parents when our children are young because it is too late when they are teenagers. It is always better to start off being tough, setting firm limits and then easing up, rather than the reverse. Over the years, the parents whom I have seen who were easygoing when the children were small and then proceeded to get tough when they were full-grown encountered violent reactions. This principle is easy to see in other contexts. At the movies we feel compassion for the hard-bitten commander who has driven his men hard but who eventually shows his soft side. But we don't really believe it when an easygoing boss starts to talk tough. We know him too well; we don't believe it. Parental authority has to be established before parental lenience.

One last observation about parenting. In talking with parents around the country, I have noticed one quality in those parents who seem to succeed with their teenagers. It is a clinical observation, and I don't have research data to support it; I offer it for what it is worth. Almost without exception, the parents who succeed with their teenagers have a sense of humor. Parents who have a sense of humor don't take themselves or their teenagers too seriously and tend to see the trials and tribulations of adolescence as just that—a troublesome time of life that will pass. Such parents accord teenagers a special place, and they can balance the headaches teenagers provoke against the pleasures of their special charm and creativity.

What Schools Can Do

There are many things that schools can do to help young people grow in a constructive and positive way. But there is one thing in particular they can do that will immediately alleviate many of the problems that were discussed in Chapter 7. This action can be taken in large cities and in small towns, in big-school systems and in little ones. It will not require the

206

building of new buildings or the training or retraining of teachers. Yet this action will boost teachers' morale and students' motivation. Academic achievement will improve, and lawlessness and dropping out will decline.

What is this magic action? It is simple and straightforward. In elementary schools, in junior high and high schools, in urban schools and suburban schools, in large schools and small schools, only one change needs to be made: *reduce class size to eighteen or fewer students.*

What do parents pay for when they send their children to a private school or college? It is not superior teaching, because the teachers in private schools are no better or worse than those in public schools, and this holds true at the university level, too. Institutions such as the University of California at Berkeley, the University of Michigan, and the University of Texas have faculty every bit as distinguished as the small private colleges and universities. Are parents then paying for prestige? Perhaps some are, but the majority are paying for the superior education that accompanies small class size.

To be sure, in some countries such as England and Japan the class size is large and educational achievement remains high. But those are relatively homogeneous cultures in which the children come to school already heavily conditioned to a single social norm and thus ready to accept the teacher's authority as an extension of parental authority. But in our society, where the parental authority is unlikely to be firmly established and young people are subject to numerous claims on their allegiance, large classes lead to anarchy.

The benefits of smaller class size should be obvious. For one, the teacher has less paperwork and can devote more time to each student. This means that the teacher can individualize more, give more homework assignments, and give homework a more careful reading. In small classes, teachers can modify the curriculum and be more innovative. In addition, children get to know one another and the teacher better, and that promotes constructive growth by comparison and contrast. Moreover, children develop a greater sense of self-worth because they see that the teacher takes time for them and their work.

Finally, it is easier to assimilate children with special needs and gifted children into a smaller classroom than into a large one.

Many research studies support the beneficial effects of small class size. But perhaps the best evidence comes from the natural experiment that has been conducted in New Hampshire over the last decade or so:

> For the 10th time in the last 10 years, New Hampshire students achieved the highest average scores on the Scholastic Aptitude Test of those of any state, according to figures released recently by the United States Department of Education. Yet New Hampshire ranks 50th, dead last, in state aid to public schools. It is also 48th in salaries paid to teachers, Federal statistics show, although the state authorities insist the situation is not that bad. . . .
>
> There are other factors that may contribute to New Hampshire's S.A.T. scores. Class size tends to be small. In Hopkinton's red brick high school the average is 10 students to a teacher.[2]

In New Hampshire children are not hurried. It is one of the few states in the nation that provides "readiness" classes for children who have completed kindergarten but who are not yet ready for first grade.

To be sure, reducing class size may cause some reshuffling. Some special-needs teachers may have to teach regular classes, and school psychologists and counselors as well as some administrators may have to do the same. These are not serious hardships for anyone and might even be beneficial. By simply reducing class size we can improve the quality of education across the land without great cost or personal or social upheaval. We as parents need to choose this alternative above all others and then insist that our local schools implement it.

Prevention: The Media

The media encourages growth by substitution and the construction of a patchwork self by thrusting adulthood upon teenagers, by portraying them as adultified children. These portrayals are meant to reflect the world we live in today. Although this is true to a certain extent, it encourages the very trend it seeks to depict. Columnist Chris Chase writes:

> "Blame It on Rio" is part of a new wave of movie comedies—"Risky Business," which brought us a high school boy joyously embracing pimphood—that make no moral judgments about the sexual ways of teenagers on the loose and on the pill.
>
> Teenagers think it is about time. It's the grown-ups who are surprised. They've always thought lying and sneaking around and dabbling in adultery was reserved for them.
>
> Actually, teenage sex may be replacing car chases in the movies. . . . Take the high school lovers in "Reckless." Never mind that he looks thirty, and when he gets irritable, he burns down his house. She finds him irresistible, so irresistible she does it with him on the floor of their high school boiler room.
>
> And the boy in "Risky Business" finds a not-so-cheap thrill (courtesy of a professional lady) on a commuter train. And the kid in "Class" is attacked by his best friend's mother in an elevator riding up and down the outside of a building.[3]

Organizations such as Action for Children's Television and the National Council for Children and Television are working to promote better programming for children and youth, but it is an uphill battle. Censorship is not really the answer. What is needed is a concerted effort by those in the media and those concerned with the welfare of children and youth to stem the flow of trash for kids. Many people in the entertainment industry are genuinely concerned about the direction television and the movies have taken and are working to lessen the violence and sex and to improve the images of teenagers and adults portrayed on the small and the large screen. We have to support their efforts by not encouraging children and teenagers to spend their time and money on the shoddy fare so widely offered today.

Stress Management

Even young people who are able to attain a healthy sense of self and identity can be overwhelmed by the magnitude of psychological stress in today's society. We can help them not only by encouraging the constructive development of personality but also by providing additional strategies for dealing with the three major stress situations. Some useful ways for handling each of these kinds of stress are outlined below.

Type A: Foreseeable and Avoidable Dangers

The emotions associated with Type A stress are anxiety and worry. As we saw in Chapter 2, worry is a product of thinking in a new key and the accompanying ability to think about the future. Many young people who can foresee a danger and recognize its avoidability may still worry about the mechanics of it. A girl knows that a boy she does not like is going to ask her out, and she knows that she is going to refuse, but she still worries about how to do this without hurting his feelings. Another teenager has let homework pile up for so long that his or her grades will fall. Still another is worried about the pressures from one friend to ignore another whom the first friend wants to punish. The teenager knows that going along with the wishes of one friend may mean losing the friendship of the other.

For all Type A situations, there is a useful formula that can reduce the related anxiety:

1. Identify the type of stress.
2. Explore your options.
3. Take action.

Teenagers can learn to identify the kind of stress situation they are facing, but sometimes they need help in exploring options. Indeed, this is where most run aground. We often have many more options than we realize. Recall the woman mentioned earlier who discovered that she had the option of "not doing" what she supposedly wanted to do.

For the girl who is worried about turning down an invitation, what are the options? Decline with dismissal ("Don't bother calling me again"); decline with encouragement ("I'm busy, but I would like to go out with you; please call again"); decline without comment ("I'm sorry, I'm busy that evening and can't go out with you"). In this instance the last response might be preferable. Teenagers often feel that they have to explain everything; in fact, by saying less they say more, but in a way that lets the other party come to his or her own conclusions.

Once the various options have been explored, the teenager has a ready course of action whenever the situation should arise and no longer need worry about that particular situation.

The teenager who has let his or her work pile up should follow the same approach. In this instance, the options are three: Don't do the work and get low grades; do the work right away; postpone doing it for a while longer. It is clear what option would be the most stress-reducing for this teenager. But here we run into a more complicated but not unusual problem. What do we do as parents if the teenager chooses to procrastinate and not do the work? The temptation, of course, is to make the teenager's problem *our* problem and to worry about what will happen if the work does not get done. It is best not to get involved in this way if possible. Rather, we should exercise our persistence, as I described earlier. We may keep reminding the teenager of the work that needs to be done. In effect our persistence must become another stress that is foreseeable and avoidable.

In this type of situation we help young people most by duplicating what happens in the world at large. On the job no one is going to give employees special rewards for doing what they were hired to do. Employers are going to insist that the job be done. If the teenager, like the employee, has a problem meeting a certain responsibility, we should not make the teenager's problem our problem. In deciding what to do in a particular case, we should consider how we would handle such a problem if it occurred at our place of business.

Although this may seem hard-hearted, it has the greatest benefit for the teenager and for us. If we make a habit of taking on the teenager's responsibilities because we dislike the consequences of failure for him or her, we deprive the young person of a crucial experience of becoming an adult. The consequences of failure are more severe for adults, and we should not set up our youngsters for painful lessons they could have learned in their early years with relatively little trouble. In addition, if we become involved in our teenager's problems, we may continue to be involved in those problems for much longer than we bargained for.

Type B: Unforeseeable and Unavoidable Stress

Some stresses can't be predicted or avoided. The best protection against these stresses for teenagers, as for all of us, is a perspective on life as a whole. Many different writers have addressed this type of stress. William James wrote, "Be willing to have it so. Acceptance of what has happened is the first step in overcoming the consequences of any misfortune. The Greek philosopher Epictetus wrote almost twenty centuries ago, "There is only one way to happiness, and that is to cease worrying about things which are beyond our will." These two writers express the same essential truth: some things in life cannot be changed. Both sayings are simple and honest truths that can make difficult moments easier.

Young people are receptive to the wisdom of adults. How many of us, now that we are grown, continue to repeat sayings we heard from our parents and grandparents, sayings that still serve as well when things are difficult? I still recall that when I was young and things had not gone the way I had hoped, my mother used to say, "It will be all right; this too will pass." When a Type B stress is caused by other persons, a few good curses are in order, too. One of my mother's I like a lot is the following: "He should grow like an onion with his head in the dirt!"

Giving teenagers stories, sayings, poems, as well as a curse or two can help them over life's rough spots. They may not immediately acknowledge our words or their benefit; in fact, they may make fun of what we have to say. But this is another of those times when we have to be persistent and not dissuaded. When teenagers are confronted with situations that are unforeseeable and unavoidable, we have to help them learn, in Dale Carnegie's words, "to cooperate with the inevitable."[4]

One final bit of wisdom speaks to both Type A and Type B stress situations; it was written by the theologian Reinhold Niebuhr.

> God grant me the serenity
> To accept the things I cannot change,
> The courage to change the things I can,
> And the wisdom to know the difference.

Type C: Foreseeable and Unavoidable Stress

In most cases, what is foreseeable and unavoidable has to do with actions we have to take or work we have to perform. The best way to help young people deal with this type of stress is to encourage good work habits. There are several constructive work habits that we can pass on to young people to help them manage the stress of foreseeable but unavoidable tasks.

The first habit is to do first the thing you wish to do least. Once young people have learned to do what they least want to do, getting at the other tasks seems like a reward. In addition, this habit teaches us to assign priorities to the various things we have to do. It also contributes to self-motivation, because we get to do the things we want to do after we have done the things we didn't want to do. Learning this habit takes effort in the beginning, but once acquired, it brings many rewards later in life. The person who works in this way is respected as efficient, reliable, and conscientious.

A second habit is to plan the work to be done each day

and to set specific goals. When he was a teenager, the psychologist Jean Piaget wrote a book entitled *Research*, which outlined a plan of work for his whole life. To a remarkable degree, he fulfilled that plan. He set himself a daily goal as well. He rose at five o'clock each morning and wrote the equivalent of five printed pages. He did that throughout his life and authored or edited more than a hundred books and over a thousand articles. George Bernard Shaw also set himself the goal of writing five pages each day. He did this for nine years while working as a bank cashier and piling up rejection slips. He earned only thirty dollars from his writing during those nine years.

A third good work habit is to do each task as if it were our last, to give every job we do, whether small or large, important or unimportant, our full attention and effort. It troubles me to go into a store and see young employees who are more interested in talking to peers than in doing the job they were hired to do. I recall, in contrast, watching a janitor at Logan International Airport in Boston sweeping the floor and collecting the trash. It was not a prestigious job, to say the least, but he obviously took pride in what he was doing and was pleased at the neat, clean look of the trash barrel after he had emptied and relined it. This man knew the secret of taking pride in one's work. The pride comes not from the prestige associated with the particular job, but rather from the knowledge that we have done the very best we know how. We give our best. If we could instill this and the other two work habits in our young people, the stress of Type C situations would become the stress of pleasure and satisfaction.

Type D: Unforeseeable but Avoidable Stress

Up till now, I have avoided talking about a fourth type (D) of stress situation, the unforeseeable but avoidable stress. At first, this sort of stress would seem to be unmanageable. How can we avoid something that is unforeseeable? The answer is religious faith. In most faiths, at least one prayer asks "God [to] deliver us from evil." We cannot foresee what evils will overcome us in this world, but we know that no one is spared. The emotion produced by the unforeseeable and avoidable is awe and reverence.

This kind of stress is different from the others, for it presents a logical contradiction that requires, in Kierkegaard's term, a leap of faith. It is our connection with what is transcendent. I believe that we can help young people deal with this form of stress, which they inevitably discover on their own, by providing them with a religious orientation. The various cults that have filled the vacuum left by traditional religious institutions are not geared to the needs of youth and are exploitative; they provide an instant "off the rack" identity. Young people cannot attain a completely integrated sense of self and identity without an understanding of that which goes beyond self and society. Institutional religion must once again extend its ministry to youth, not only to provide a bulwark against cults, but to fulfill perhaps the most important part of its ministry, the spiritual needs of youth.

Many writers have not been kind to religion. Freud called it an illusion, and Marx called it the opiate of the people. But religion speaks to a deep and abiding need in all of us, or it could not have survived. Religion provides a perspective beyond ourselves and our world that helps us to manage the existential problem of realizing our significance and place in the universe. If we do not have a religious faith ourselves, we should not deny it or denigrate it to our offspring. And if we have a faith, we should share it without imposing it. Our responsibility as parents includes opening this part of life to our children and preparing them to make their own decisions.

These are difficult times for adults and teenagers alike. It is easy at such times to put oneself ahead of others. But we have to remember that our individuality, our identity, is a hard-won social achievement. It is not inborn. Our individuality is a product of our social experience, not something separate and apart from it. We acquired our individuality, our sense of self, through the labors of parents who set standards, limits, and rules so that we could discover who and what we were and how we could relate in meaningful and productive ways to others.

That was our birthright acknowledged and nutured by our parents. We cannot, should not, dare not, deny that birthright to our teenagers. We must once again allow teenagers a place in our society. We must once again be adults to children and youth. And we must once again give evidence of our faith in them and in the future. For only then will teenagers regain a place to be young and find a place to go when they are all grown up.

Appendix

Services for Troubled Teenagers

Alcohol and Drug Abuse

National Federation of Parents for Drug Free Youth
P.O. Box 57217
Washington, DC 20037

National Institute on Drug Abuse
P.O. Box 2305
Rockville, MD 20852

Palmer Drug Abuse Program
(213) 989-0902

Straight Talk
c/o Drug Fair, Inc.
6295 Edsall Rd.
Alexandria, VA 22314

Parent Self-Help Groups

Toughlove
Community Service Foundation
P.O. Box 70
Sellersville, PA 18960

Parents Anonymous
22330 Hawthorne Blvd., #208
Torrance, CA 90505
Hotline (crisis counseling and information available 24 hours a day, seven days a week)
(800) 352-0386 (in California)
(800) 421-0353 (elsewhere)

Parents and Friends of Gays
P.O. Box 24528
Los Angeles, CA 90024

Parental Stress, Inc.
(800) 632-8188 (in Massachusetts)
(617) 742-7573 (elsewhere)
A twenty-four-hour service for parents experiencing crises with their children.

Runaway Services

For the name of a runaway or teen crisis shelter in your area, write:

National Youth Work Alliance
1346 Connecticut Avenue, N.W.
Washington, DC 20036

National Runaway Switchboard
(800) 621-4000
(A toll-free service offering crisis help and referrals nationwide)

Suicide Prevention

Almost every state in the Union now has one or more suicide hotlines and suicide prevention centers. Your local phone operator will give you the number for the hotline in your area.

Notes

CHAPTER 1: TEENAGERS IN CRISIS

1. N. Cobb, "Who's Getting High on What?," *Boston Globe*, October 10, 1982.
2. M. Zelnick and J. Kantner, "Sexuality, Contraception and Pregnancy among Young Unwed Females in the United States," *Research Reports*, Commission on Population Growth and the American Future, vol. 1 (Washington, D.C.: Government Printing Office, 1980).
3. C. L. Tishler, "Adolescent Suicide: Prevention, Practice and Treatment," *Feelings and Their Medical Significance* 23, no. 6 (November–December 1981).
4. C. Murphy, "Kids Today," *Wilson Quarterly*, Autumn 1982.
5. "Shelters and Streets Draw Throw-away Kids," *New York Times*, June 3, 1983.
6. E. Erikson, *Childhood and Society* (New York: Norton, 1950).
7. J. Piaget, *The Psychology of Intelligence* (London: Routledge & Kegan Paul, 1950).
8. E. L. Boyer, *Highschool* (New York: Harper & Row, 1983), p. 4.
9. D. Yankelovich, *New Rules* (New York: Bantam, 1981).
10. Ibid., p. 7.
11. Ibid., p. 3.
12. J. Naisbitt, *Megatrends* (New York: Warner, 1982).
13. E. Goodman, "The Turmoil of Teenage Sexuality," *Ms.*, July 1983, pp. 37–41.
14. H. Hesse, *Steppenwolf* (New York: Rinehart, 1963), p. 24.
15. J. J. Rousseau, *Emile* (New York: Basic Books, 1979).
16. E. Z. Friedenberg, *The Vanishing Adolescent* (New York: Dell, 1959), pp. 21–22.

CHAPTER 2:   THINKING IN A NEW KEY

1. Quoted in E. C. Winship, *Reaching Your Teenager* (Boston: Houghton-Mifflin, 1983).
2. J. Piaget, *The Psychology of Intelligence* (London: Routledge & Kegan Paul, 1950).
3. *MAD*, September 1983, pp. 12–13.
4. J. Bealty, Jr., *Matthew Looney and the Space Pirates* (New York: Avon, 1972), p. 14.
5. J. Blume, *Are You There God? It's Me, Margaret* (New York: Dell, 1970), pp. 27–28.
6. Quoted in Winship, *Reaching Your Teenager.*
7. Ibid.
8. "Helping a Teenager Grow Up Gradually," *Boston Globe*, July 8, 1983.
9. J. Betancourt, *Am I Normal?* (New York: Avon, 1983), pp. 17–20.
10. D. Elkind, *The Child's Reality: Three Developmental Themes* (Hillsdale, N. J.: Erlbaum, 1979). G. R. Adams and R. M. Jones, "Imaginary Audience Behavior: A Validation Study," *Early Adolescence* 1 (1981): 1–10.
11. P. Danziger, *The Cat Ate My Gymsuit* (New York: Dell, 1973), p. 14.
12. D. Elkind and R. Bowen, "Imaginary Audience Behavior in Children and Adolescents," *Developmental Psychology* 15 (1979): 38–44.
13. A. Markey, "Be Your Body's Buddy," *Teen*, February 1983.
14. J. Knowles, *A Separate Peace* (New York: Macmillan, 1959), p. 1.
15. Blume, *Are You There God? It's Me, Margaret*, p. 94.

CHAPTER 3:   PERILS OF PUBERTY

1. H. Katchadourian, *The Biology of Adolescence* (San Francisco: Freeman & Sons, 1977).
2. J. Norman and M. Harris, *The Private Life of the American Teenager* (New York: Rawson-Wade, 1981).
3. P. Danziger, *The Cat Ate My Gymsuit* (New York: Dell, 1973), p. 7.
4. Katchadourian, *The Biology of Adolescence.*
5. Quoted in E. C. Winship, *Reaching Your Teenager* (Boston: Houghton-Mifflin, 1983).
6. L. H. Gross (ed.), *The Parents' Guide to Teenagers* (New York: Macmillan, 1981).
7. J. Blume, *Are You There God? It's Me, Margaret* (New York: Dell, 1970), pp. 116–117.
8. W. A. Marshall and J. M. Tanner, "Variations in the Pattern of Pubertal Changes in Girls," *Archives of Disease in Childhood* 44 (1969): 291–301.
9. C. Morley, *Kitty Foyle* (New York: Queens House, 1977; originally published 1939), p. 32.

10. Blume, *Are You There God? It's Me, Margaret,* p. 100.
11. Katchadourian, *The Biology of Adolescence.*
12. Quoted in Winship, *Reaching Your Teenager.*
13. Gross, *The Parents' Guide to Teenagers.*
14. Katchadourian.
15. Gross.
16. Quoted in Winship.
17. J. Betancourt, *Am I Normal?* (New York: Avon, 1983), p. 41.
18. G. S. Hall, *Confessions of a Psychologist* (New York: Appleton, 1924), p. 82.
19. Norman and Harris, *The Private Life of the American Teenager.*
20. J. Blume, *Then Again, Maybe I Won't* (New York: Dell, 1971), pp. 83–84.
21. D. Ephron, *Teenage Romance* (New York: Ballantine, 1981), pp. 115–116.
22. Quoted in A. Heron (ed.), *One Teenager in Ten* (Boston: Alyson, 1983).
23. Ibid.
24. S. Freud, "The Passing of the Oedipus Complex," in *The Collected Papers of Sigmund Freud,* vol. 2 (London: Hogarth, 1953).
25. Ibid.
26. A. Freud, *The Ego and the Mechanisms of Defense* (New York: International Universities Press, 1946).
27. B. F. Steele, "Abusive Fathers," in S. H. Gath, A. R. Gurvitch, and J. M. Ross (eds.), *Father and Child* (Boston: Little, Brown, 1981).
28. Ibid.
29. Quoted in M. Jackson and J. Jackson, *Your Father's Not Coming Home Anymore* (New York: Ace Books, 1981).

CHAPTER 4: PEER SHOCK

1. R. Alexander, "Valley Girls Aren't Just in California," *New York Times,* September 17, 1982.
2. S. A. Toth, *Blooming: A Small Town Girlhood* (Boston: Little, Brown, 1981), pp. 62–63.
3. C. McCullers, *The Member of the Wedding* (New York: Bantam, 1983; first published 1946), p. 137.
4. E. Goffman, *Strategic Interactions* (Philadelphia: University of Pennsylvania Press, 1969).
5. E. Goffman, *Frame Analysis* (New York: Harper, 1974).
6. S. Jackson, *Come Along with Me* (New York: Viking, 1960).
7. J. Blume, *Then Again, Maybe I Won't* (New York: Dell, 1971).
8. A. Muro, "Cecilia Rosas," *New Mexico Quarterly* 4 (Winter 1964–1965).
9. Ibid.
10. Quoted in J. Norman and M. Harris, *The Private Life of the American Teenager* (New York: Rawson-Wade, 1981).

11. J. Knowles, *A Separate Peace* (New York: Macmillan, 1959), pp. 44–45.
12. "Dear Jill," *Teen Magazine*, February 1983.
13. D. Weir, "Shyness," *Young Miss*, February 1983.
14. C. Robertson, *A Summer to Remember* (New York: Silhouette, 1983), pp. 161–162.
15. Weir, "Shyness."
16. V. Randall, "Waiting for Jim," in T. W. Gregory (ed.), *Adolescence in Literature* (New York: Longman, 1978).
17. M. Zelnick and J. Kantner, "Sexuality, Contraception and Pregnancy among Young Unwed Females in the United States," *Research Reports*, Commission on Population Growth and the American Future, vol. 1 (Washington, D.C.: Government Printing Office, 1980).
18. Norman and Harris, *The Private Life of the American Teenager*.
19. D. Ephron, *Teenage Romance* (New York: Ballantine, 1981), pp. 95, 103.
20. Quoted in A. Hess, *Teenage Sexuality* (New York: Ballantine, 1981).

CHAPTER 5: VANISHING MARKERS

1. S. Kierkegaard, *Stages on Life's Way* (Princeton: Princeton University Press, 1945).
2. P. Charren and M. Sandler, *Changing Channels* (Reading, Mass.: Addison-Wesley, 1983), p. 33.
3. H. Whittemore, "The Competitors," *Parade Magazine*, April 11, 1982.
4. L. Langway, E. Shannon, D. Shirley, and J. Taylor, "Young Fu," *Newsweek*, January 17, 1983.
5. N. Postman, *The Disappearance of Childhood* (New York: Delacorte, 1982).
6. J. Norman and M. Harris, *The Private Life of the American Teenager* (New York: Rawson-Wade, 1981).
7. Charren and Sandler, *Changing Channels*, p. 63.
8. E. Stein, "Have Horror Films Gone Too Far?," *New York Times*, June 20, 1982.
9. S. Bedell, "Junior Knows Best: TV's View of Children Today," *New York Times*, September 19, 1982.
10. Ibid.
11. Quoted in Bedell.
12. G. D. Goldberg, "A Producer Responds," *Television and Children*, Spring 1983, pp. 15–16.
13. V. Canby, "Youth Has Its Day as Movies Face Reality," *New York Times*, October 24, 1982.
14. Ibid.
15. Ibid.
16. "Disney Hopes to Spice up Profits," *New York Times*, February 19, 1984.
17. D. Ravitch, *The Troubled Crusade* (New York: Basic Books, 1983), p. 323.

CHAPTER 6: FAMILY PERMUTATIONS

1. J. Naisbitt, *Megatrends* (New York: Warner, 1982).
2. G. B. Spanier and P. C. Slick, "Marital Instability in the United States: Some Correlates and Recent Changes," *Family Relations* 30 (1981): 329–338.
3. M. Jackson and J. Jackson, *Your Father's Not Coming Home Anymore* (New York: Ace Books, 1981).
4. J. Norman and M. Harris, *The Private Life of the American Teenager* (New York: Rawson-Wade, 1981).
5. Ibid.
6. Ibid.
7. Ibid.
8. F. C. Kleen, "Stepfamilies Growing Common, Pose a Host of Problems," *Wall Street Journal*, December 23, 1982.
9. Ibid.
10. Ibid.
11. Ibid.
12. Quoted in A. Wood, "Stepparents: How to Deal with Them," *Seventeen*, February 1983.
13. Ibid.
14. Quoted in Kleen, "Stepfamilies."
15. Ibid.
16. C. Tietze, "Teenage Pregnancy: Looking Ahead to 1984," *Family Planning Perspectives* 10 (1978): 205–207.
17. A. G. Crawford and F. F. Furstenberg, "Teenage Sexuality, Pregnancy and Child Welfare," paper presented at Conference on School Age Pregnancies and Parenthood, Belvin Conference Center, Maryland, May 23–26, 1982.
18. Ibid.
19. J. Trussel, "Economic Consequences of Teenage Childbearing," *Family Planning Perspectives* 8, no. 4 (1976): 184–190.
20. J. Huber, "Married Students vs. Married Dropouts," *Phi Delta Kappan* 52 (1970): 115–116. J. J. Card and L. L. Wise, "Teenage Mothers and Teenage Fathers: The Impact of Early Childbearing on the Parents' Personal and Professional Lives," *Family Planning Perspectives* 10 (1978): 199–205.
21. A. Landers, "Grandfather Feels Ashamed," *Boston Globe*, July 24, 1983.
22. A. B. Elster and M. E. Lamb, "Adolescent Fathers: Their Influence on Child Development," paper presented at Conference on School Age Pregnancies and Parenthood, Belvin Conference Center, Maryland, May 23–26, 1982.

CHAPTER 7: SCHOOLS FOR SCANDAL

1. R. B. Sheridan, *The School for Scandal*, in C. W. Eliot (ed.), *The Harvard Classics*, vol. 18 (New York: Collier, 1909).
2. See, e.g., D. P. Gardner and Y. W. Larsen, *A Nation at Risk* (National Commission on Excellence in Education, U.S. Department of Education, 1983); E. L. Boyer, *Highschool* (New York: Harper & Row, 1983).
3. Gardner and Larsen, *A Nation at Risk*, pp. 8–9.
4. Boyer, *Highschool*.
5. M. Jackson and B. Jackson, *Doing Drugs* (New York: Martins/Marek, 1983).
6. Boyer, *Highschool*, p. 44.
7. Ibid., p. 46.
8. K. O'Dell, "More of Us from 3–34 Are in School," *U.S.A. Today*, March 21, 1983.
9. D. Ravitch, *The Troubled Crusade* (New York: Basic Books, 1983), p. 327.
10. Ibid.
11. Ibid.
12. M. Barnacle, "Why They Hate School," *Boston Globe*, September 17, 1982.
13. Quoted in Boyer, *Highschool*.
14. Ibid.
15. Ibid.
16. Ibid.
17. M. Adler, *The Poidea Proposal* (New York: Macmillan, 1982).
18. Gardner and Larsen, *A Nation at Risk*, pp. 18–19.
19. D. Ephron, *Teenage Romance* (New York: Ballantine, 1981).
20. Boyer, *Highschool*, p. 162.
21. Ibid., p. 163.
22. Ibid., p. 154.
23. J. Coleman, *High School and Beyond: A National Longitudinal Study for the 1980's*, survey conducted by the National Research Center, Chicago, for the National Center for Education Statistics, 1980.
24. Quoted in E. B. Fiske, "Etzioni Wants to Shift Focus to Students," *New York Times*, November 1, 1983.

CHAPTER 8: STRESS, IDENTITY, AND THE PATCHWORK SELF

1. H. Selye, *The Stress of Life* (New York: McGraw-Hill, 1976).
2. Quoted in K. McCoy, *Coping with Teenage Depression* (New York: New American Library, 1982).
3. Ibid.
4. Ibid.

5. Quoted in M. Jackson and B. Jackson, *Doing Drugs* (New York: Martins/ Marek, 1983).
6. Quoted in McCoy, *Coping with Teenage Depression.*
7. Quoted in J. Norman and M. Harris, *The Private Life of the American Teenager* (New York: Rawson-Wade, 1981).
8. Ibid.
9. Quoted in McCoy, *Coping with Teenage Depression.*

CHAPTER 9: TEENAGE REACTIONS TO STRESS

1. D. Yankelovitch, *New Rules.* (New York: Bantam, 1981).
2. "I'm Scared a War Will Start—You Know 1,2,3, Boom," *Reading Eagle* (Reading, Pa.), January 19, 1982.
3. K. McCoy, *Coping with Teenage Depression* (New York: New American Library, 1982).
4. E. L. Boyer, *Highschool* (New York: Harper & Row, 1981).
5. Quoted in J. Norman and M. Harris, *The Private Life of the American Teenager* (New York: Rawson-Wade, 1981).
6. Quoted in McCoy, *Coping with Teenage Depression.*
7. N. Cobb, "Who's Getting High on What?," *Boston Globe*, October 10, 1982.
8. Ibid.
9. Ibid.
10. W. Cross, *Kids and Booze* (New York: E. P. Dutton, 1979).
11. Ibid.
12. G. Collins, "U.S. Social Tolerance of Drugs Found on Rise," *New York Times*, March 21, 1983.
13. M. Jackson and J. Jackson, *Your Father's Not Coming Home Anymore* (New York: Ace Books, 1981).
14. L. H. Gross, *The Parents' Guide to Teenagers* (New York: Macmillan, 1981).
15. C. L. Tishler, "Adolescent Suicide: Prevention, Practice and Treatment," *Feelings and Their Medical Significance* 23, no. 6 (November–December 1981).
16. Quoted in M. K. Seff, "Anatomy of a Suicide Attempt," *Boston Globe*, November 20, 1981.
17. R. C. Casper, "Treatment Principles in Anorexia Nervosa," in Feinstein et al., *Adolescent Psychiatry* (Chicago: University of Chicago Press, 1982).
18. D. Arnold, "Karen Carpenter's Death Draws Attention to Anorexia," *Boston Globe*, February 6, 1983.
19. Casper, "Treatment Principles."
20. E. Landau, *Why Are They Starving Themselves?* (New York: Julian Messner, 1983).
21. Quoted in McCoy, *Coping with Teenage Depression.*

22. York and Hochte, *Toughlove* (Garden City, N.Y.: Doubleday, 1982).
23. "Shelters and Streets Draw Throw-away Kids," *New York Times,* June 3, 1983.
24. Ibid.
25. Ibid.
26. Ibid.
27. Ibid.
28. D. Rader, "Children on the Run," *Parade Magazine,* September 5, 1982.
29. Ibid.

CHAPTER 10:   HELPING TEENAGERS COPE

1. R. W. Emerson, "Essays and English Traits," in C. W. Eliot (ed.), *The Harvard Classics,* vol. 5 (New York: Collier, 1909).
2. *New York Times,* February 3, 1984.
3. C. Chase, "Gosh, Please Don't Blame It on Rio," *New York Times,* February 26, 1984.
4. D. Carnegie, *How to Stop Worrying and Start Living* (New York: Pocket Books, 1948).

Index

Index